STECK-VAUGHN

TABE®
Fundamentals

Focus on Skills

Reading

LEVEL D

2nd Edition

HOUGHTON MIFFLIN HARCOURT
Supplemental Publishers

www.SteckVaughn.com
800-531-5015

D1089348

Photo Credits: P iv: ©Bluestone Productions/SuperStock
Royalty Free; 2: ©Photodisc/Getty Images Royalty Free;
4: ©Veer Royalty Free; 45: ©Bettmann/CORBIS.

Illustrations: Pp. 22, 72, 76, 80 Francine Mastrangelo; pp. 41, 46,
53, 55, 64, 82 Bob Novak.

Reviewers

Victor Gathers
Regional Coordinator of Adult Services
New York City Department of Education
Brooklyn Adult Learning Center
Brooklyn, New York

Brannon Lentz
Assistant Director of Adult Education/Skills Training
Northwest Shoals Community College
Muscle Shoals, Alabama

Jean Pierre-Pipkin, Ed.D.
Director of Beaumont I.S.D. Adult Education
Cooperative Consortium
Beaumont, Texas

ISBN-13: 978-1-4190-5356-6
ISBN-10:   1-4190-5356-6

© 2009, 2004 Steck-Vaughn, an imprint of HMH Supplemental Publishers Inc.

Steck-Vaughn is a trademark of HMH Supplemental Publishers Inc.

TABE® is a trademark of McGraw-Hill, Inc. Such company has neither endorsed nor authorized this publication.

Printed in the United States of America.

7 8 9 1689 15 14 13 12
4500342632

Contents

To the Learner

Congratulations on your decision to study for the TABE! You are taking an important step in your educational career. This book will help you do your best on the TABE. You'll also find hints and strategies that will help you prepare for test day. Practice these skills—your success lies in your hands.

What Is the TABE?

TABE stands for the Tests of Adult Basic Education. These paper-and-pencil tests, published by McGraw-Hill, measure your progress on basic skills. There are five tests in all: Reading, Mathematics Computation, Applied Mathematics, Language, and Spelling.

TABE Levels M, D, and A

Test	Number of Items	Suggested Working Time (in minutes)
1 Reading	50	50
2 Mathematics Computation	25	15
3 Applied Mathematics	50	50
4 Language	55	39
5 Spelling	20	10

Test 1 Reading

This test measures basic reading skills. The main concepts covered by this test are word meaning, critical thinking, and understanding basic information.

Many things on this test will look familiar to you. They include documents and forms necessary to your everyday life, such as directions, bank statements, maps, and consumer labels. The test also includes items that measure your ability to find and use information from a dictionary, table of contents, or library computer display. The TABE also tests a learner's understanding of fiction and nonfiction passages.

Test 2 Mathematics Computation

Test 2 covers adding, subtracting, multiplying, and dividing. On the test you must use these skills with whole numbers, fractions, decimals, integers, and percents.

The skills covered in the Mathematics Computation test are the same skills you use daily to balance your checkbook, double a recipe, or fix your car.

Test 3 Applied Mathematics

The Applied Mathematics test links mathematical ideas to real-world situations. Many things you do every day require basic math. Making budgets, cooking, and doing your taxes all take math. The test covers pre-algebra, algebra, and geometry, too. Adults need to use all these skills.

Some questions will relate to one theme. Auto repairs could be the subject, for example. The question could focus on the repair schedule. For example, you know when you last had your car repaired. You also know how often you have to get it repaired. You might have to predict the next maintenance date.

Many of the items will not require you to use a specific strategy or formula to get the correct answer. Instead this test challenges you to use your own problem-solving strategies to answer the question.

Test 4 Language

The Language test asks you to analyze different types of writing. Examples are business letters, resumes, job reports, and essays. For each task, you have to show you understand good writing skills.

The questions fit adult interests and concerns. Some questions ask you to think about what is wrong in the written material. In other cases, you will correct sentences and paragraphs.

Test 5 Spelling

In everyday life, you need to spell correctly, especially in the workplace. The spelling words on this test are words that many people misspell and words that are commonly used in adult writing.

Test-Taking Tips

1. Read the directions very carefully. Make sure you read through them word for word. If you are not sure what the question says, ask the person giving the test to explain it to you.

2. Read each question carefully. Make sure you know what it means and what you have to do.

3. Read all of the answers carefully, even if you think you know the answer.

4. Make sure that the reading supports your answer. Don't answer without checking the reading. Don't rely only on outside knowledge.

5. Answer all of the questions. If you can't find the right answer, rule out the answers that you know are wrong. Then try to figure out the right answer. If you still don't know, make your best guess.

6. If you can't figure out the answer, put a light mark by the question and come back to it later. Erase your marks before you finish.

7. Don't change an answer unless you are sure your first answer is wrong. Usually your first idea is the correct answer.

8. If you get nervous, stop for a while. Take a few breaths and relax. Then start working again.

How to Use *TABE Fundamentals*

Step-by-Step Instruction In Levels M and D, each lesson starts with step-by-step instruction on a skill. The instruction contains examples and then a test example with feedback. This instruction is followed by practice questions. Work all of the questions in the lesson's practice and then check your work in the Answers and Explanations in the back of the book.

The Level A books contain practice for each skill covered on the TABE. Work all of the practice questions and then check your work in the Answers and Explanations in the back of the book.

Reviews The lessons in Levels M and D are grouped by a TABE Objective. At the end of each TABE Objective, there is a Review. Use these Reviews to find out if you need to review any of the lessons before continuing.

Performance Assessment At the end of every book, there is a special section called the Performance Assessment. This section is similar to the TABE test. It has the same number and type of questions. This assessment will give you an idea of what the real test is like.

Answer Sheet At the back of the book is a practice bubble-in answer sheet. Practice bubbling in your answers. Fill in the answer sheet carefully. For each answer, mark only one numbered space on the answer sheet. Mark the space beside the number that corresponds to the question. Mark only one answer per question. On the real TABE, if you have more than one answer per question, they will be scored as incorrect. Be sure to erase any stray marks.

Strategies and Hints Pay careful attention to the TABE Strategies and Hints throughout this book. Strategies are test-taking tips that help you do better on the test. Hints give you extra information about a skill.

Setting Goals

On the following page is a form to help you set your goals. Setting goals will help you get more from your work in this book.

Section 1. Why do you want to do well on the TABE? Take some time now to set your short-term and long-term goals on page 3.

Section 2. Making a schedule is one way to set priorities. Deadlines will help you stay focused on the steps you need to take to reach your goals.

Section 3. Your goals may change over time. This is natural. After a month, for example, check the progress you've made. Do you need to add new goals or make any changes to the ones you have? Checking your progress on a regular basis helps you reach your goals.

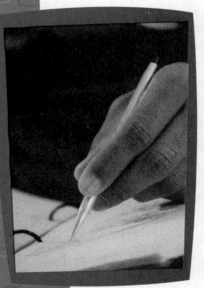

For more information on setting goals, see Steck-Vaughn's *Start Smart Goal Setting Strategies*.

1. Set Your Goals

What is your long-term goal for using this book?

_____

_____

_____

_____

Complete these areas to identify the smaller steps to take to reach your long-term goal.

Content area	What I Know	What I Want to Learn
Reading	_____	_____
Language	_____	_____
Spelling	_____	_____
Math	_____	_____
Other	_____	_____

2. Make a Schedule

Set some deadlines for yourself.

For a 20-week planning calendar, see Steck-Vaughn's *Start Smart Planner*.

Goals	Begin Date	End Date
_____	_____	_____
_____	_____	_____
_____	_____	_____
_____	_____	_____
_____	_____	_____

3. Celebrate Your Success

Note the progress you've made. If you made changes in your goals, record them here.

_____

_____

_____

_____

To the Learner • 3

To the Instructor

About TABE

The Tests of Adult Basic Education are designed to meet the needs of adult learners in ABE programs. Written and designed to be relevant to adult learners' lives and interests, this material focuses on the life, job, academic, and problem-solving skills that the typical adult needs.

Because of the increasing importance of thinking skills in any curriculum, *TABE Fundamentals* focuses on critical thinking throughout each TABE Objective.

The TABE identifies the following thinking processes as essential to learning and achieving goals in daily life:

✦ Gather Information
✦ Organize Information
✦ Analyze Information
✦ Generate Ideas
✦ Synthesize Elements
✦ Evaluate Outcomes

Test 1 Reading

The TABE measures an adult's ability to understand home, workplace, and academic texts. The ability to construct meaning from prose and visual information is also covered through reading and analyzing diagrams, maps, charts, forms, and consumer materials.

Test 2 Mathematics Computation

This test covers whole numbers, decimals, fractions, integers, percents, and algebraic expressions. Skills are carefully targeted to the appropriate level of difficulty.

Test 3 Applied Mathematics

This test emphasizes problem-solving and critical-thinking skills, with a focus on the life-skill applications of mathematics. Estimation and pattern-recognition skills also are important on this test.

Test 4 Language

The Language test focuses on writing and effective communication. Students examine writing samples that need revision, with complete-sentence and paragraph contexts for the various items. The test emphasizes editing, proofreading, and other key skills. The contexts of the questions are real-life settings appropriate to adults.

Test 5 Spelling

This test focuses on the words learners most typically misspell. In this way, the test identifies the spelling skills learners most need in order to communicate effectively. Items typically present high-frequency words in short sentences.

Uses of the TABE

There are three basic uses of the TABE:

Instructional

From an instructional point of view, the TABE allows instructors to assess students' entry levels as they begin an adult program. The TABE also allows instructors to diagnose learners' strengths and weaknesses in order to determine appropriate areas to focus instruction. Finally, the TABE allows instructors and institutions to monitor learners' progress.

Administrative

The TABE allows institutions to assess classes in general and measure the effectiveness of instruction and whether learners are making progress.

Governmental

The TABE provides a means of assessing a school's or program's effectiveness.

The National Reporting System (NRS) and the TABE

Adult education and literacy programs are federally funded and thus accountable to the federal government. The National Reporting System monitors adult education. Developed with the help of adult educators, the NRS sets the reporting requirements for adult education programs around the country. The information collected by the NRS is used to assess the effectiveness of adult education programs and make necessary improvements.

A key measure defined by the NRS is educational gain, which is an assessment of the improvement in learners' reading, writing, speaking, listening, and other skills during their instruction. Programs assess educational gain at every stage of instruction.

NRS Functioning Levels	Grade Levels	TABE (7–8) scaled scores
Beginning ABE Literacy	0–1.9	Reading . . . . 367 and below Total Math . . . . 313 and below Language . . . . . 392 and below
Beginning Basic Education	2–3.9	Reading . . . . 368–460 Total Math . . . . 314–441 Language 393–490
Low Intermediate Basic Education	4–5.9	Reading . . . . 461–517 Total Math . . . . 442–505 Language 491–523
High Intermediate Basic Education	6–8.9	Reading . . . . 518–566 Total Math . . . . 506–565 Language 524–559
Low Adult Secondary Education	9–10.9	Reading . . . . 567–595 Total Math . . . . 566–594 Language 560–585

According to the NRS guidelines, states select the method of assessment appropriate for their needs. States can assess educational gain either through standardized tests or through performance-based assessment. Among the standardized tests typically used under NRS guidelines is the TABE, which meets the NRS standards both for administrative procedures and for scoring.

The three main methods used by the NRS to collect data are the following:

1. **Direct program reporting,** from the moment of student enrollment
2. **Local follow-up surveys,** involving learners' employment or academic goals
3. **Data matching,** or sharing data among agencies serving the same clients so that outcomes unique to each program can be identified.

Two of the major goals of the NRS are academic achievement and workplace readiness. Educational gain is a means to reaching these goals. As learners progress through the adult education curriculum, the progress they make should help them either obtain or keep employment or obtain a diploma, whether at the secondary school level or higher. The TABE is flexible enough to meet both the academic and workplace goals set forth by the NRS.

Using *TABE Fundamentals*

Adult Basic Education Placement

From the outset, the TABE allows effective placement of learners. You can use the *TABE Fundamentals* series to support instruction of those skills where help is needed.

High School Equivalency

Placement often involves predicting learners' success on the GED, the high school equivalency exam. Each level of *TABE Fundamentals* covers Reading, Language, Spelling, and Applied and Computational Math to allow learners to focus their attention where it is needed.

Assessing Progress

Each TABE skill is covered in a lesson. These lessons are grouped by TABE Objective. At the end of each TABE Objective, there is a Review. Use these Reviews to find out if the learners need to review any of the skills before continuing.

At the end of the book, there is a special section called the Performance Assessment. This section is similar to the TABE test. It has the same number and type of questions. You can use the Performance Assessment as a timed pretest or posttest with your learners, or as a more general review for the actual TABE.

Steck-Vaughn's *TABE Fundamentals* Program at a Glance

The charts on the following page provide a quick overview of the elements of Steck-Vaughn's *TABE Fundamentals* series. Use this chart to match the TABE objectives with the skill areas for each level. This chart will come in handy whenever you need to find which objectives fit the specific skill areas you need to cover.

Steck-Vaughn's *TABE Fundamentals* Program at a Glance

TABE OBJECTIVE

TABE Objective	Level M — Reading	Level M — Language and Spelling	Level D — Reading	Level D — Language and Spelling	Level A — Reading, Language, and Spelling
Reading					
Interpret Graphic Information	✦		✦		✦
Words in Context	✦		✦		✦
Recall Information	✦		✦		✦
Construct Meaning	✦		✦		✦
Evaluate/Extend Meaning	✦		✦		✦
Language					
Usage		✦		✦	
Sentence Formation		✦		✦	✦
Paragraph Development		✦		✦	✦
Punctuation and Capitalization		✦		✦	✦
Writing Conventions		✦		✦	✦
Spelling					
Vowel		✦		✦	✦
Consonant		✦		✦	✦
Structural Unit		✦		✦	✦

TABE Objective	Level M — Math Computation	Level M — Applied Math	Level D — Math Computation	Level D — Applied Math	Level A — Computational and Applied Math
Mathematics Computation					
Addition of Whole Numbers	✦				
Subtraction of Whole Numbers	✦				
Multiplication of Whole Numbers	✦		✦		
Division of Whole Numbers	✦		✦		
Decimals	✦		✦		✦
Fractions	✦		✦		✦
Integers			✦		✦
Percents			✦		✦
Orders of Operation			✦		✦
Applied Mathematics					
Number and Number Operations		✦		✦	✦
Computation in Context		✦		✦	✦
Estimation		✦		✦	✦
Measurement		✦		✦	✦
Geometry and Spatial Sense		✦		✦	✦
Data Analysis		✦		✦	✦
Statistics and Probability		✦		✦	✦
Patterns, Functions, Algebra		✦		✦	✦
Problem Solving and Reasoning		✦		✦	✦

Lesson 1 Index

An index is located at the end of most books. It contains an alphabetized list of the book's contents and the page numbers where specific information can be found. If you know how to use an index, you will be able to locate information in a book quickly and efficiently.

Example **Look at this section of an index page from a car service manual. Suppose your car's clutch is loose and you want to fix it. On what page would you find information on how to adjust the clutch? Circle the page number.**

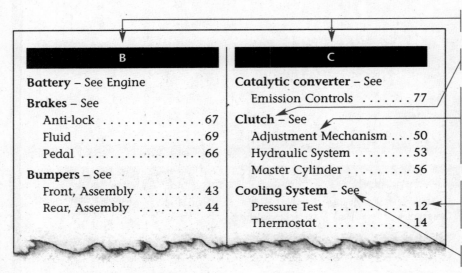

B

Battery – See Engine

Brakes – See
  Anti-lock 67
  Fluid 69
  Pedal 66

Bumpers – See
  Front, Assembly 43
  Rear, Assembly 44

C

Catalytic converter – See
  Emission Controls 77

Clutch – See
  Adjustment Mechanism . . . 50
  Hydraulic System 53
  Master Cylinder 56

Cooling System – See
  Pressure Test 12
  Thermostat 14

Entries in an index are arranged in alphabetical order.

Index listings are topics or sub-topics.

Sometimes an index topic has a lot of information about it so it will be broken down into sub-topics. Sub-topics are listed under the topic to which they belong. Sub-topics are listed in alphabetical order.

The page number where the information can be found is directly to the right of each topic or sub-topic.

The word *See* directs you from a topic to another topic or sub-topic.

Information on clutch adjustments is on page 50. The number 50 is to the right of the sub-topic "adjustment mechanism" under the topic "Clutch."

Test Example

Refer to the car service manual index above. Then do number 1. Circle the letter of the correct answer.

1 If you want to read about how to repair your anti-lock brakes, on which page will you look for that information?

A 69

C 33

B 66

D 67

When trying to locate specific information in an index, think of possible general topics under which it might be listed. Specific information is often listed as a sub-topic of a general topic.

1 **D** Page 67 has information about anti-lock brakes. Option A is not correct because page 69 has information about brake fluid. Option B is not correct because page 66 has information about the brake pedal. Page 33 is not listed (option C).

Study this index page from a home improvement book. Then answer numbers 1 through 4 by circling the letter of the best answer.

R	
Refrigerator	 103
Roofs – See	
Framing	 310
Installing Insulation	 331

S	
Siding – See	
Patching	 35
Removing	 34
Sinks – See	
Bathroom	 228
Kitchen	 225
Skylights	 426

Subfloor – See	
Attic	 82
Basement	 12
Repairing	 84
Suspended Ceilings	 208

T	
Templates – See	
Flooring Installation	 80
Framing Windows	 187
Tile – See	
Cutter	 17
Vinyl Tiles	 33
Trim – See	
Cutting	 41
Moldings	 43
Nailing	 46

1 If you want to repair a small hole on the vinyl siding of a house, on which page will you look?

A 84

B 35

C 34

D 33

2 Which of these cannot be found on this index page?

F Trim

G Templates

H Tile

J Two-slot receptacle

3 Which of these is listed on page 208?

A vinyl tiles

B framing windows

C suspended ceilings

D flooring installation

4 Suppose you want to install a new drain in the bathroom sink. On which page will you find information on how to do this?

F 228

G 225

H 331

J 84

Check your answers on page 86.

Lesson 2 | Reference Sources

Reference sources are used to find information. Being familiar with all kinds of reference sources will help you decide which is most useful when you need to look up something. On the TABE you will have to decide which reference source has the information being asked for in the question. You will also be asked how to give credit to a reference that is written into a report.

Example If you were looking for a famous saying from Dr. Martin Luther King, Jr.,

which would be the best reference source to use?_____

Look at the chart below to review the different types and purposes of common reference sources.

Reference Source	What It Is	Why It Is Used
almanac	a calendar-like book that gives facts and statistics about government, economics, sports, and other topics	to quickly locate facts and figures about topics
anthology	a collection of writing	to read a collection of the same kind of writing, such as short stories or poems
atlas	a book of maps, sometimes with historical and statistical information	to get geographic information or to locate a place
book of quotations	a book that has sayings from famous people	to quickly find a quote
encyclopedia	a book that has articles on subjects, arranged in alphabetical order	to get brief explanations of things in our world
magazine	a publication that has articles about different topics of interest	to read for pleasure or to find out about topics in the news

Famous sayings from Martin Luther King, Jr., would be in a book of quotations.

Example If you wanted to use a quote from a book for a report you are writing,

how would you give the author credit? _____

_____

Any time you quote any author you should give credit. **To give credit, note the book source in a footnote at the bottom of the page.** A footnote has information about the book such as the title, author, and the page number on which the quote was found.

Test Example

Read the question. Circle the letter of the best answer.

1 When writing a paper, if you use the exact words of an author you should

A put a line under the quote in your paper

B copy the quote in the bibliography

C footnote the source of the quote

D write the author's name on the title page of your paper

1 C Option C is the correct answer. Just putting a line under a quote (option A) would not show where it came from. Copying the quote (option B) would also not tell where the quote came from. Option D is not correct because the quote source does not belong on a title page.

Practice

Answer numbers 1 through 6 by circling the letter of the best answer.

1 You would probably find the most sayings by Thomas Jefferson in

A an atlas

B an encyclopedia

C a book of quotations

D an anthology of short stories

2 The fastest way to find out where Charlottesville is in the state of Virginia would be to look in

F an atlas

G an almanac

H a magazine

J a book of quotations

3 If you directly quote the author of a book in a report you are writing about Thomas Jefferson, you should

A highlight the quotation

B use a footnote to credit the source

C write the author's name at the top of the report

D include all the books written by the author in the bibliography

4 Which of these would probably be the best source of information about the inventions of Thomas Jefferson?

F *Architectural Design*

G *The Writer's Notebook*

H *Thomas Jefferson's Inventions*

J *The History of the Copy Machine*

5 If you wanted a brief explanation of Jefferson's major contributions, in which of these reference sources would you look?

A an atlas

B an encyclopedia

C a book of quotations

D an anthology of short stories

6 Jefferson designed his own hilltop house in Charlottesville, Virginia. If you were interested in buying land and building a house in Charlottesville, which of these reference sources would you use?

F an atlas

G an encyclopedia

H *Charlottesville Real Estate Weekly*

J *The History of Virginia*

Check your answers on page 86.

Consumer Materials

The TABE asks you to answer questions based on materials for consumers—people who use goods and services. A label, such as one that gives nutrition facts, is one type of consumer material. To understand labels, you need to analyze and use the information they provide.

Example **Read the paragraph and study the nutrition label for the frozen beef stir-fry meal. Do you think this meal is a good choice for Leah?**

Leah wants a quick, portable meal that she can eat during her half-hour lunch break at work. Her doctor told her to limit the amount of fat she eats. He suggested that a good lunch would provide no more than 350 calories, fewer than 700 milligrams of sodium, and at least five grams of dietary fiber. Leah found a $3 frozen beef stir-fry meal at the supermarket.

Leah likes Asian food, especially stir fry. She can store this low-fat meal in the lunchroom and cook it in the microwave there. Her lunch break is 30 minutes; the meal cooks in five minutes. The meal and a carton of skim milk fall within her lunch budget. Leah makes a list of requirements and checks off each item by comparing it to the label.

Nutrition Facts		
Serving Size 1 package		
Servings Per Container 1		
Calories 290		Calories from Fat 35
		% Daily Value*
Total Fat 4g		6%
Saturated Fat 1g		5%
Trans Fat 0g		
Polyunsaturated Fat 1.5g		
Monounsaturated Fat 1g		
Cholesterol 30mg		10%
Sodium 640mg		27%
Potassium 550mg		16%
Total Carbohydrate		15%
Dietary Fiber 4g		16%
Sugars 19g		
Protein 17g		
Vitamin A	60% * Vitamin C	25%
Calcium	6% * Iron	8%

* Percent Daily Values are based on a 2,000 calorie diet. Your daily values may be higher or lower depending on your calorie needs.

Study the nutrition facts label and compare it to Leah's checklist below. The meal fails to meet one of her requirements. Which one? _____

___Maximum lunch expense: $4
___Maximum calories: 350
___Maximum daily salt intake: 2000 mg
___Minimum dietary fiber: 5
___Lunch break: 30 minutes

Did you answer that the meal did not meet the fiber requirement? High-fiber foods are filling and contribute to good health. Leah will have to decide if she can add extra fiber to her breakfast or dinner meals.

Test Example

Study the nutrition facts label and Leah's checklist. Then circle the letter of the best answer.

1   Which part of the meal does <u>not</u> meet Leah's requirements?

A   cost

B   dietary fiber

C   sodium

D   calories

TABE Strategy

Pay attention to words that are underlined in test questions. The word *not* is an important word in this question.

1 B Leah's doctor suggested a minimum of 5 grams of fiber; the meal has only 4. She can afford the meal within her $4 lunch budget. The meal meets her salt-intake guidelines and has fewer than 350 calories.

Practice

First read the paragraph about Jorge and Leo. Then analyze the five nutrition facts labels. Finally, answer numbers 1 through 4 by circling the letter of the best answer.

Jorge needs to pack a lunch for his seven-year-old son, Leo, who is going on a class field trip. Leo has asked for a sandwich, a beverage, some raw vegetables, and a cookie. Jorge knows the foods Leo likes best, but he also wants Leo to have a healthful diet. Jorge has these sandwich ingredients and beverages in the house.

Fat-Free Milk

Nutrition Facts
Serving Size 1 cup

Servings Per Container 16
Calories 90   Calories from Fat 0
                                    % Daily Value*
Total Fat 0g   0%
   Saturated Fat 0g   0%
   Trans Fat 0g
Cholesterol 5mg   0%
Sodium 125mg   5%
Total Carbohydrate   4%
   Dietary Fiber 0g   0%
   Sugars 12g
Protein 8g

Vitamin A   10% • Vitamin C   4%
Calcium   30% • Vitamin D   25%

* Percent Daily Values are based on a 2,000 calorie diet. Your daily values may be higher or lower depending on your calorie needs.

Cranberry-Blueberry Juice

Nutrition Facts
Serving Size 1 cup

Servings Per Container 8
Calories 140   Calories from Fat 0
                                    % Daily Value*
Total Fat 0g   0%
Sodium 35mg   1%
Total Carbohydrate   11%
   Dietary Fiber 0g   0%
   Sugars 30g
Protein 0g

Vitamin C   100%

* Percent Daily Values are based on a 2,000 calorie diet. Your daily values may be higher or lower depending on your calorie needs.

Cheddar Cheese

Nutrition Facts
Serving Size 1 oz

Servings Per Container 16
Calories 110   Calories from Fat 80
                                    % Daily Value*
Total Fat 9g   14%
   Saturated Fat 6g   30%
   Trans Fat 0g
Cholesterol 25mg   9%
Sodium 410mg   17%
Total Carbohydrate   0%
   Dietary Fiber 0g   0%
   Sugars 0g
Protein 6g

Vitamin A   6% • Calcium   20%

* Percent Daily Values are based on a 2,000 calorie diet. Your daily values may be higher or lower depending on your calorie needs.

Roast Beef Luncheon Meat

Nutrition Facts
Serving Size 6 slices

Servings Per Container 4
Calories 60   Calories from Fat 20
                                    % Daily Value*
Total Fat 2g   3%
   Saturated Fat 1g   5%
   Trans Fat 0g
Cholesterol 30mg   10%
Sodium 520mg   22%
Total Carbohydrate   0%
   Dietary Fiber 0g   0%
   Sugars 0g
Protein 10g

Iron   8%

* Percent Daily Values are based on a 2,000 calorie diet. Your daily values may be higher or lower depending on your calorie needs.

Natural Creamy Peanut Butter

Nutrition Facts
Serving Size 2 tbsp

Servings Per Container 14
Calories 210   Calories from Fat 150
                                    % Daily Value*
Total Fat 16g   25%
   Saturated Fat 2.5g   12%
   Trans Fat 0g
Cholesterol 0mg   0%
Sodium 120mg   5%
Total Carbohydrate 6g   2%
   Dietary Fiber 2g   9%
   Sugars 1g
Protein 8g

Iron   2%

* Percent Daily Values are based on a 2,000 calorie diet. Your daily values may be higher or lower depending on your calorie needs.

1 The lunch that provides Leo with the most calcium includes

A peanut butter and milk

B roast beef and juice

C cheese and milk

D peanut butter and juice

2 What is one reason Jorge would <u>not</u> consider packing a roast beef sandwich?

F The roast beef contains less protein than cheese or peanut butter.

G The roast beef has more sodium than cheese or peanut butter.

H The roast beef is higher in calories than cheese or peanut butter.

J The roast beef is higher in fat than cheese or peanut butter.

3 Which of the foods meets Leo's total daily requirement of a vitamin or mineral?

A cranberry-blueberry juice

B cheddar cheese

C peanut butter

D milk

4 Which important dietary need is <u>not</u> met by four of the five food choices?

F fat

G protein

H carbohydrates

J dietary fiber

Check your answers on page 86.

Amy's family is planning to visit Graceland, home of rock and roll legend Elvis Presley. They would also like to see other Memphis attractions during their one-week vacation. The travel brochure below lists some points of interest. Study the brochure. Then answer numbers 1 through 3 by circling the letter of the best answer.

Memphis Highlights

Memphis Music and Heritage Festival
Families enjoy musicians, dancers, artists, cooks, talkers, and performers.
Labor Day weekend

Children's Museum of Memphis
Children explore science, math, health, art, and more with hands-on, interactive exhibits.
Mon.–Sat. 9am–5pm
Sun. 12 noon–5 pm

Chucalissa Museum and Archaeological Site
Exhibits show the prehistory of the Mid-South and modern Southeastern Indian cultures to young and old alike.
Tues.–Sat. 9am–5 pm
Sun. 1–5 pm (April–Nov.)

The Cotton Museum
Adults and schoolchildren learn the story of the cotton industry and its influences on the region with exhibits, programs, and a research library.
Mon.–Sat. 10am–5 pm
Sun. 12 noon–5 pm

Fire Museum of Memphis
People of all ages explore the history of firefighting in Memphis and fire safety information through interactive exhibits.
Mon.–Sat. 9 am–5 pm

Lichterman Nature Center
In this urban nature center, families can explore a three-story-high forest boardwalk filled with plants, birds, reptiles, amphibians, and mammals.
Tues.–Thurs. 9 am–4 pm
Fri.–Sat. 9 am–5 pm

1 Because Amy's family loves animals, they will *most likely* visit the

A Fire Museum of Memphis

B Lichterman Nature Center

C Cotton Museum

D Chucalissa Museum and Archaeological Site

2 Why might Amy's family not attend the Memphis Music and Heritage Festival?

F It appeals only to people who love music.

G It costs too much.

H It is difficult to find.

J It takes place only one weekend a year.

3 In what way is the Children's Museum different from the other attractions?

A It is just for children.

B It is located in Memphis.

C It has exhibits.

D It is educational.

Study this part of an index page from a book about Elvis Presley. Then answer number 4.

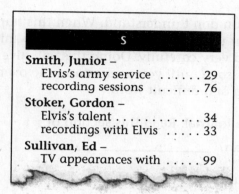

S
Smith, Junior –
Elvis's army service 29
recording sessions 76
Stoker, Gordon –
Elvis's talent 34
recordings with Elvis 33
Sullivan, Ed –
TV appearances with 99

4 If Amy wants to find out more about Elvis's recording sessions with Junior Smith, on which page would she look?

F 29

G 33

H 76

J 99

Amy wants to read more about Elvis. What reference sources can she use? Answer questions 5 and 6 by circling the letter of the best answer.

5 Where can Amy find famous sayings by Elvis?

A in an almanac

B in an encyclopedia

C in a book of quotations

D in an anthology

6 A biography of Elvis Presley would *most likely* be titled

F *The Life and Times of the King of Rock 'n' Roll*

G *From the Blues to Rock 'n' Roll: A Musical History*

H *Famous Southerners of the Twentieth Century*

J *Peanut Butter and Bananas: An Elvis Cookbook*

Check your answers on page 87.

Lesson 4 Same Meaning

When you read, you sometimes come across words you don't understand. When this happens, there are ways to figure out what a word means without using a dictionary. You can do this by reading the other words and sentences around the word very carefully. Doing this will give you clues about the meaning of the word. If you study a passage until you understand the overall meaning, you can often figure out the specific meaning of a difficult word.

Example Tracy has been writing about her dreams in a journal. Read this section of her journal. What does the word *pursued* mean? _____

> I woke up this morning with my heart pounding. I dreamed that I was being pursued by a black bear.

Did you write that *pursued* means being chased or followed? By reading the first sentence, you can conclude that the action in Tracy's dream made her feel scared. A black bear chasing a scared person would make the person's heart race and face sweat. If you substituted either *chased* or *followed* for the word *pursued*, the sentence would still fit with the meaning of the passage: I dreamed that I was being *chased* by a black bear.

Example Read this sentence. It also uses the word *pursued*. What does *pursued* mean in this sentence? _____

> George pursued a degree in nursing.

Did you write *worked toward*? In some test questions, there may be more than one correct meaning in the answer choices. In order to choose the *best* answer, carefully read *how* the word is used in the passage. For example, if this meaning of the word *pursued* is substituted in the sentence from the first example, it would not make sense: I dreamed that I was being *worked toward* by a black bear.

Test Example

Read the following excerpt from Tracy's journal. Answer the question by circling the letter of the best answer.

> In my dream I was running through the woods. Tree branches brushed my face as I ran. The black bear was getting closer and closer. I could feel my knees start to buckle. Just as I was about to fall, I woke up.

1 What does the word *buckle* mean in the paragraph?

A to panic

B to rub together

C a clasp on a belt

D to bend or give way

TABE Strategy

Read every answer. Substitute each answer for the word in the sentence and choose the answer that best fits with the meaning of the sentence and the passage.

1 D The word *buckle* in this paragraph means "to bend or give way." When you are about to fall, your knees give way. "To panic" means to suddenly show fear (option A). Knees cannot show fear. Buckle does not mean "to rub together" (option B). Although buckle does mean "a clasp on a belt," that definition does not fit the meaning of the sentence (option C).

Practice

Tracy keeps a journal of her dreams by her bedside. Read this entry. Answer the questions by circling the letter of the best answer.

I remember the sound of the cool wind *whipping* by my face. Two wings, *adorned* with soft, brown feathers, stretched far to the sides of my proud, majestic body. I *scanned* the ground below, looking for any signs of movement. The urgency of my search kept me focused and *determined*. I was an eagle, caught between the freedom of floating *effortlessly* through the cold night air and the *tingle* of hunger slowly moving through the whole of my body.

1 The author says that she remembers "the sound of the cool wind *whipping* by my face." In this context, the word *whipping* means the same as

A beating

B mixing

C blowing

D singing

2 The author describes the eagle's wings as *adorned* with soft, brown feathers. Which of these means the same as the word *adorned*?

F adhered

G admired

H traveled

J decorated

3 According to the paragraph, the eagle "*scanned* the ground below, looking for any signs of movement." What does the word *scanned* mean here?

A copied

B searched

C swindled

D traversed

4 The author says "the urgency of my search kept me focused and *determined*." What does the word *determined* mean in this sentence?

F awake

G steadfast

H defeated

J delighted

5 In the paragraph, the eagle is described as "floating *effortlessly*." In this context, the word *effortlessly* means the same as

A without pain

B without warmth

C without warning

D without force

6 The last sentence mentions the "*tingle* of hunger." What does the word *tingle* mean?

F a cold sensation

G a sudden movement

H a prickling sensation

J a feeling of alertness

Check your answers on page 87.

Lesson 5   Opposite Meaning

Knowing the meaning of a word can help you identify another word that means the opposite. Sometimes TABE questions ask you to choose a word with the opposite, or a completely different, meaning. For example, a word that means the opposite of *energetic* is *lazy*. Another pair of opposite words, or antonyms, is *wealthy* and *poor*.

Example **Read this paragraph. Think of the meaning of the underlined word. Which**

word means the opposite of *fortunate*? _____

> LeRoy considers himself the most <u>fortunate</u> man on the planet. Last week, he would have fallen off a high beam at work, but an alert coworker seized his tool belt and pulled him to safety. Later that day, he found a $20 bill in the parking lot. Yesterday, he won a barbecue grill in a store's grand opening drawing.

To figure out the opposite meaning of a word, first define the word. *Fortune* is another word for *good luck*. *Fortunate*, therefore, means *lucky*. Then think of a word that means the opposite of *lucky*. **The opposite of *fortunate* is *unlucky*.**

Now locate the word *seized* in the second sentence of the
paragraph. Then write a word or combination of words that
means the opposite of *seized*. _____

How did you arrive at your answer? Did you first identify the meaning of *seized*? When we *seize* something, we take hold of it quickly and firmly. The opposite of *seized*, then, is *let go* or *dropped*. **Did you write *released, relinquished, dropped,* or a similar word?**

Test Example

Read the paragraph. Answer the question by circling the letter of the best answer.

1   LeRoy didn't fall because his coworker *seized* his tool belt and pulled him to safety. Which of these words means the <u>opposite</u> of *seized*?

   A   grabbed

   B   clasped

   C   released

   D   gripped

1   C   *Seized*, in this sentence, means "took hold of firmly and quickly." The opposite of *seized* is *released*. *Grabbed* (option A), *clasped* (option B), and *gripped* (option D) are words that mean the same as *seized*.

Read the article. Then answer questions 1 through 4 by circling the letter of the best answer.

Does Luck Exist?

"You have the best luck: a job promotion, a big pay raise, and a huge new office!" "What bad luck! My car broke down, my cell phone didn't work, and I missed my job interview."

The dictionary defines *luck* as "a force that brings good fortune or great problems." The definition suggests that an intangible, unseen force outside a person's control causes good or horrible things to happen: a car breakdown, a phone failure, a missed interview.

Thomas Jefferson might not have agreed! The following quote is credited to the former president: *"I'm a great believer in luck, and I find the harder I work the more I have of it."* Based on the quote, Jefferson believes that *luck* or, in this context, *good luck* is simply the result of hard work. He might have suggested that job success comes from effort, and car and phone failures result from lack of care or faulty equipment.

Luck or effort—which controls your life? You decide.

1 The first paragraph mentions a job *promotion*. Which of the following words means the <u>opposite</u> of *promotion*?

A advancement

B upgrade

C demotion

D commotion

2 Paragraph two describes luck as the result of "an *intangible,* unseen force outside a person's control." A word that means the <u>opposite</u> of *intangible* is

F touchable

G abstract

H unreal

J terrible

3 Thomas Jefferson is identified as a *former* president in paragraph three. Which word means the <u>opposite</u> of *former*?

A current

B deceased

C previous

D respected

4 Paragraph three lists *faulty* equipment as a possible cause of car and phone failures. Words that mean the <u>opposite</u> of *faulty* are

F defective or impaired

G unfit or flawed

H ancient or old

J sound or functioning

Check your answers on pages 87–88.

Lesson 6 | Appropriate Word

Some TABE questions provide a passage for you to read. Following the passage will be a sentence about the passage in which one word is missing. You will be asked to supply an appropriate word to complete the sentence. An appropriate word is one that is suitable or makes sense in the sentence. You are already an expert at finding appropriate words. Every time you talk or write, you search for just the right, or appropriate, word that will help others understand what you want to say.

Example **Read this paragraph. What is the paragraph about?**

_____

Drip, drip, drip…. Do you recognize this sound? Yes, it's the sound of a leaky faucet. Although it's annoying, the leak is so small that it isn't worth calling a plumber, right? You might be astonished to learn the giant cost of a tiny drip.

Test Example

Read the sentence and the question to decide on an appropriate word for the blank.

The expense of a water leak is a big _____ to homeowners.

1 Which word shows that people are unpleasantly surprised by the cost of a water leak?

    A gift

    B joke

    C shock

    D puzzle

1 **C** *Shock* means "surprise or dismay." The words *gift* (option A), *joke* (option B), and *puzzle* (option D) do not suggest an unpleasant surprise.

Read the article. Answer the questions by circling the letter of the best answer.

On average, one drop of water is approximately 0.3 milliliter; consequently, one liter of water contains 3,000 drops and a gallon consists of 11,350 drops. If one faucet in your home leaks at a rate of one drop per second, you will pay for 7 gallons of wasted water every day and 2,777 gallons each year. (Imagine this—you could have taken 55 baths with that water!)

Consider, then, the cost of a community of 100,000 homes—each with one leaky faucet. Each day, 760,898 gallons of water pours down the drains without helping a single person. In the course of one year, this community wastes 277,727,873 gallons of water.

1 Read the sentence and the question to decide which word goes in the blank.

If communities continue to waste water, they may need to find new _____ of water.

Which word completes the idea that other water supplies may be necessary?

A uses

B sources

C kinds

D flavors

2 Read the sentence and the question to decide which word goes in the blank.

Homeowners should _____ leaky faucets to save both money and water.

Which word completes the idea that people should stop faucets from leaking?

F notice

G purchase

H repair

J install

3 Read the sentence and the question to decide which word goes in the blank.

In communities with water shortages, some governments _____ the amount of water people can use.

Which word completes the idea that governments limit water usage?

A restrict

B produce

C increase

D ignore

4 Read the sentence and the question to decide which word goes in the blank.

If everyone works to _____ water, everyone will have enough for years to come.

Which word completes the idea that people should use water wisely?

F consume

G conserve

H connect

J construct

Check your answers on page 88.

Read this passage. Answer the questions by circling the letter of the best answer.

Sunday Supper

Sundays throughout my childhood were spent at my grandparents' house where supper was served at exactly two o'clock. My memory of the aroma of slow-baked, spice-covered chicken makes my stomach growl even now. In the distance, I could hear the sound of my mother and my grandmother talking, muffled only by a closed kitchen door. Their low voices seemed to blend together.

When the feast emerged from the kitchen, we were all called to the table. My brother and I sat at the far end, where we would indulge ourselves in the glory of our drumsticks. The conversation between the adults seemed to drag on in slow motion. I often slithered halfway off my chair to see the view from under the table. From there, I could see the thick folds of my grandmother's legs. Her dark stockings fell just under her knees. They stopped at a certain place that made me feel unsettled. I held back the desire to reach over and pull them up.

Dessert was cake and fruit eaten around the living room coffee table. My favorite fruit was, and still is, ripe pomegranate. I don't know what I liked better, opening the fruit or eating it. Watching my grandfather open a pomegranate was like watching a sculptor carving his way around a block of wood, slowly revealing the artwork that lay hidden beneath its layers. His teeth would pierce the skin, and I remember seeing little red spurts of sweet juice squirt from the edges of his mouth. Then he would place his thumbs under the exposed opening. He took a deep breath, clenched his teeth, and ripped the pomegranate apart. For that one moment in time, he was the toughest man in the world. My brother and I mimicked my grandfather, tearing our sections into smaller pieces with great force and strength.

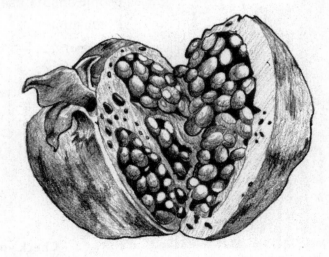

1 According to the passage, the author remembers "the *aroma* of slow-baked, spice-covered chicken." What does the word *aroma* mean here?

   A taste

   B scent

   C sight

   D flavor

2 In the passage, the author recalls "My brother and I sat at the far end, where we would *indulge* ourselves in the glory of our drumsticks." What does the word *indulge* mean here?

   F to eat

   G to cover

   H to gratify

   J to embrace

3 According to the passage, "the feast *emerged* from the kitchen." Which word means the opposite of the word *emerged*?

   A originated

   B escaped

   C proceeded

   D disappeared

4 The passage says that the conversation "seemed to *drag* on in slow motion." What does the word *drag* mean here?

   F pull

   G search

   H move slowly

   J move quickly

Read the sentence and the question to decide which word goes in the blank.

5 The writer has _____ memories of childhood suppers at his grandparents' home.

Which word completes the idea that the writer clearly remembers Sunday suppers?

   A vivid

   B vague

   C dreadful

   D occasional

6 The author says his grandfather "would place his thumbs under the *exposed* opening." Which word means the opposite of the word *exposed*?

   F concealed

   G opened

   H revealed

   J peeled

7 The author mentions the feeling of being *unsettled* by the sight of his grandmother's stockings. Which word means the opposite of the word *unsettled*?

   A comfortable

   B uneasy

   C not paid

   D happy

8 The last sentence says, "My brother and I *mimicked* my grandfather." What does the word *mimicked* mean here?

   F amused

   G imitated

   H irritated

   J introduced

Check your answers on pages 88–89.

Lesson 7 Details

It is important to pay close attention to details when reading TABE passages. Details are the facts or the specific information that makes up a story. They tell *who, what, why, where, when,* and *how*. Noticing details helps you understand what you are reading.

Example **Read the paragraph below. Three of the details are underlined.**

> Native Americans lived peacefully in North America for hundreds of years. They first came in contact with European settlers in the early 1600s. While the Europeans had more sophisticated weapons technology, the Native Americans used bows and arrows.

This paragraph gives details that answer these questions: *Who? Where? When?* and *What?*

Find the detail in the paragraph that answers the question: "Where did they live?" Put the answer in the empty box.

Detail Question	Answer
Who is the passage about?	Native Americans
Where did they live?	
When did they first come in contact with European settlers?	early 1600s
What did they use?	bows and arrows

The answer, North America, is in the first sentence of the paragraph. When you read, try to notice names, places, dates, and other facts. If a *who, what, why, where, when,* and *how* word is used in a TABE question, underline it. Then look back at the paragraph to find the answer.

Test Example

Read the paragraph. Answer the question by circling the letter of the best answer.

> Native Americans of the Plains got most of what they needed to survive from the buffalo. Buffalo meat provided food. The hide was used to make teepees and clothing. Tools and weapons were made from bones, and rope was made from hair.

TABE Strategy

Underline the word *what* in the question and refer back to the paragraph to find the answer.

1 For what purpose did the Native Americans use buffalo hair?

   A to make rope   C to make clothing

   B to make teepees   D to make weapons

Practice

Read the passage. Answer the questions by circling the letter of the best answer.

The early Native Americans of the Plains traveled and hunted on foot. When these nomadic tribes moved, they used dogs to pull sleds with their belongings. Families could own only as much as their dogs could pull.

In 1541, Spanish explorers introduced horses to North America. The Native Americans cherished horses. Many Native Americans called horses "sky dogs" in their languages. The Native Americans thought the strange animals were large dogs, sent as a gift from the Great Spirit of the sky.

The introduction of the horse increased the supply of food and improved mobility for the Native Americans. Hunting became more successful with horses. Using horses, hunters could keep up with a moving herd of buffalo. A man with a fast horse could bring home more buffalo to feed his family. Horses could also pull heavier loads than the dogs could pull. Families could now own larger teepees and fill them with more supplies.

1 According to the passage, who brought horses to North America?

A the sky dogs

B the Great Spirit

C the Native Americans

D the Spanish explorers

2 What method of travel did the early Native Americans use?

F They walked.

G They rode dogs.

H They rode horses.

J They rode in wagons.

3 According to the passage, why were horses cherished?

A They were beautiful creatures.

B They were brought by the Spanish.

C They improved hunting and traveling.

D They were thought to be related to dogs.

4 According to the passage, how were horses used?

F to train dogs

G to pull supplies

H to guard the teepees

J to carry the children

5 Which of the following probably explains why horses were called "sky dogs"?

A They liked to chase dogs.

B They were compared to birds in the sky.

C They were believed to have fallen from the sky.

D They resembled dogs and were thought to be a gift from a sky spirit.

Check your answers on page 89.

Sequence

The sequence of a story is the order in which the events happen. Knowing how to tell what comes first, second, third, and so on will help you to understand how a story unfolds. Most stories begin with the first event in the sequence of events and end with the last event. Sequence words can help you to understand the order in which events happen within a story. The TABE will have questions in which you will need to determine the sequence of events in a story.

Example Read the paragraph. As you read, pay attention to the underlined sequence words that show the order of events. Underline the event that happened after Lance Armstrong won the Iron Kids Triathlon.

Lance Armstrong was a natural athlete at an early age. At age 13, he won the Iron Kids Triathlon. <u>Then</u> he became a professional triathlete at age 16. Although Lance was a strong runner and swimmer, his favorite thing to do was race a bike. <u>After</u> graduating from high school, he decided to devote all of his time and energy to competitive cycling. In 1992, Lance finished 14th in the Olympic Games. Many wins <u>later</u>, he was named American Male Cyclist of the Year.

Did you underline the sentence that says Lance Armstrong became a professional triathlete? The sentence "Then he became a professional triathlete" comes right after the sentence "At age 13, he won the Iron Kids Triathlon." The word *then* is a sequence word that tells you that the next event is about to follow.

Test Example

Read the paragraph. As you read, pay attention to the sequence words that indicate the order of events. Answer the question by circling the letter of the best answer.

Lance's victories came to a sudden stop in 1996. He was told he had cancer. Lance was only 25 years old. After he got the bad news, he started an aggressive treatment program. First, he had three surgeries. Then he had chemotherapy. During the ordeal, Lance never gave up his cycling dreams. He missed the 1997 cycling season, but finally returned to the sport a year later.

Hint

When you read, look for sequence words such as *first, next, then, after, later,* and *finally.*

1   When did Lance have chemotherapy?

   A   after he had three surgeries

   B   when he returned to the sport

   C   after he was treated for cancer

   D   during the 1997 cycling season

1 A Chemotherapy was the second part of Lance's treatment program for cancer. According to the paragraph, he had chemotherapy *after* he had three surgeries. Option B is not correct because Lance returned to the sport of cycling *after* he was treated with chemotherapy. Option C is not correct because the chemotherapy was part of his cancer treatment, not something he did after his cancer treatment. Option D is not correct because Lance missed the 1997 cycling season while he was being treated for cancer.

Practice

Read the passage. Answer the questions by circling the letter of the best answer.

Lance Armstrong fought his way through cancer. After his recovery, he was determined to get back into racing. It was a slow, hard battle to get back into shape. First, he had to strengthen his muscles. Then he had to build up his stamina.

Many people thought that he should give up racing altogether, but Lance never quit. He got a lot of help and support from his wife, Kristin, whom he married in 1998. In July of 1999, Lance entered the most famous cycling race of all, the *Tour de France*. To everyone's surprise, he crossed the finish line far ahead of all the other riders. Lance held his arms up high at the moment of victory. He had finally made it to the top of the cycling world.

Later, in October of 1999, Lance and Kristin had a baby. They named him Luke David. Luke inspires Lance as much as Lance inspires people all over the world. Lance tells other cancer survivors, "Maybe I can prove that it's possible to return to a normal life, and maybe I can prove that it's possible to be better than you were before."

1 What happened first?

A Lance got married.

B Lance's baby was born.

C Lance got back into shape for racing.

D Lance won the Tour de France.

2 When did Lance get married?

F July of 1999

G October of 1999

H after he won the Tour de France

J before he won the Tour de France

3 When did Lance get back into shape?

A after his recovery

B before he had cancer

C after his baby was born

D after he won the Tour de France

4 What happened last?

F Lance got married.

G Lance's baby was born.

H Lance got back into shape.

J Lance won the Tour de France.

Check your answers on page 89.

Lesson 9 Stated Concepts

A stated concept is an expressed idea, opinion, or reason. It can explain why an event happens or why someone behaves in a certain way. Stated concepts can also tell a person's position on a topic. Understanding stated concepts can help you decide whether or not you agree with a particular point of view.

Example Read the paragraph below. A stated concept is underlined. Why are the makers of BGH so proud of their product? _____

_____

Today, some milk and dairy products are made with a human-made growth hormone called BGH. This hormone is injected into cows. <u>The companies that make and sell BGH boast about how farmers who use their product have increased profits. The makers of BGH claim that it increases a cow's milk production by as much as 10 to 30 percent, while the amount of food the cow eats goes up by only 5 to 10 percent.</u>

They say that their product helps farmers boost profits. The answer to the question comes from the last two sentences. The makers of BGH believe that because a cow injected with the growth hormone makes more milk, but doesn't eat a lot more, profits increase.

Some of the answer choices in the TABE may not be *directly* stated in the passage. They may be restated ideas that combine information from more than one sentence in the passage.

Test Example

Read the paragraph. Answer the question by circling the letter of the best answer.

When she became pregnant with her daughter, Sasha Miller was concerned that milk made with the help of BGH would cause harmful side effects in her baby. While some thought she was being overly careful, Sasha stood firm and permanently switched to organic milk, which does not come from cows injected with BGH. Is she right to boycott BGH dairy products? Do the hormones pose serious health risks? Sasha is joined by hundreds of other health-conscious consumers who think so. Together, they are the driving force behind sales of natural and organic products. This is now the fastest-growing segment of the food industry.

1   Which of these best describes Sasha's feelings about BGH milk?

A   She likes the flavor of BGH milk.

B   She fears that BGH could cause harm to her baby's health.

C   She is concerned about how boycotts will affect the milk industry.

D   She worries that her baby will like BGH milk better than organic milk.

1 B Sasha is concerned about the health risks of BGH. She worries that it might cause harmful side effects in her baby. The paragraph does not mention Sasha's concern about BGH milk's flavor or taste (options A and D). Sasha is boycotting BGH milk (option C).

Practice

Read the article. Answer the questions by circling the letter of the best answer.

BGH: Who Stands to Profit

Fifteen percent of American dairy cows are now injected with a growth hormone called BGH. In medical studies, BGH has been linked to cancer and other diseases in dairy cows. Even though Canada has banned the use of BGH, the United States has approved its use. Do the risks of BGH outweigh the possible benefits?

If BGH does what it advertises to do, it should increase farmers' production more than costs. Therefore, it will also raise profits. However, if BGH raises milk production, it will make the country's milk surplus grow. This country *already* produces a surplus of milk. The price of milk will drop and force many small dairy farms out of business, unless the government steps in to help.

Does more milk equal more money? It does for a select few. Obviously, the makers and sellers of BGH get the biggest payoff from BGH sales. They make an estimated $300 to $500 million each year from sales of BGH. Because the United States already produces more milk than it can use, the government will have to buy the additional milk at an estimated cost to taxpayers of $200 million or more per year.

1 According to the article, who would benefit the most from the use of BGH?

A taxpayers

B small dairy farmers

C the federal government

D companies that make and sell BGH

2 Which of these expresses a stated relationship between BGH and dairy cows?

F BGH makes cows more fertile.

G BGH makes cows more aggressive.

H Cows injected with BGH have cancer more often.

J BGH decreases the milk production of dairy cows.

3 According to the article, how will taxpayers be affected by the use of BGH?

A They will pay a lot less for milk.

B They will enjoy increased health benefits.

C They will get more choices of milk brands.

D They will have to help offset the costs of a milk surplus.

4 Which of these best represents Canada's position on BGH?

F Canada has banned the use of BGH.

G Canada's dairy farms do not have a need for BGH.

H Canada has made BGH legal to use in only some dairy cows.

J Canada's farmers can choose whether or not to use BGH.

Check your answers on pages 89–90.

Read this article from a weightlifting magazine. Answer the questions by circling the letter of the best answer.

Shock Training

You finally have a weight-training program and you've stuck with it for a while. Now what? If you want to keep seeing results, it's time for a change in your routine. Before now, you probably thought that building muscle was all about finding and sticking with the perfect workout, right? Well, it's not that simple. Building muscle is about having a few regular routines, and trying a new one every now and then.

Bodybuilders are very familiar with working through "plateaus." It's common to plateau by doing the same thing again and again. You can try increasing the amount of weights you use, but that is only part of the solution. Shock training can help you move past a plateau.

Shock training "shocks" your muscles in order to stimulate more growth. What can you do to change your regular routine? If you typically use the leg press once every five days, try using it once every ten days. Also try replacing bench presses with some flies, or adding free weights into your weight-lifting circuit. Adding an occasional variation can help give your muscles just the boost they need.

Of course, always discuss any exercise program with your doctor before beginning. 🐋

1 According to this article, how could you move past a "plateau"?

A Run 3 miles a week.

B Lift lighter weights.

C Change your routine.

D Do more repetitions.

2 What does the author suggest doing if you normally use the leg press once every five days?

F Add more weight.

G Stop using the leg press.

H Try using free weights instead.

J Try using the leg press once every ten days.

3 Which of these explains why bodybuilders sometimes stop seeing results?

A They use the weight-lifting circuit.

B They try new workouts.

C They eat more fatty foods.

D They stick to the same workouts.

4 Which of these is considered an example of "shock training"?

F adding more carbohydrates to your diet

G replacing the bench press with some flies

H inviting a friend to help you with your workout

J doing the same routine every other day for two weeks

Read this passage about Arnold Schwarzenegger, a famous bodybuilder. Answer the questions by circling the letter of the best answer.

Arnold Schwarzenegger was born in Austria on July 30, 1947. His father encouraged Arnold and his brother to play sports. He once told Arnold that he wanted him to be a star soccer player. Arnold tried to please his father, and he became a very good soccer player at school. Yet, his brother remained a far better player. Arnold was upset because his father never praised his best efforts. Arnold dropped out of soccer and started lifting weights at a local gym. At age 13, Arnold had already decided that he wanted to be the best bodybuilder in the world.

Soon Arnold was training seven days a week at the gym. One Sunday the gym was closed, but this didn't stop Arnold. He broke into the gym so that he could work out. Arnold didn't seem to mind that the heat was not on and it was the middle of winter. He kept on training.

When Arnold turned 18, he joined the Austrian Army for mandatory service. Arnold's parents hoped that the army would rid their son's passion for bodybuilding, but Arnold proved to be tougher than they had ever thought. One time he secretly left the army camp to compete in the Junior Mr. Europe Bodybuilding Competition. He won the title. Then, in 1966, Arnold entered the Mr. Universe Competition, where he won second place. The following year, he entered again and won first place. At the age of 20, Arnold became the youngest Mr. Universe in history. He had accomplished his dream.

5 According to the passage, which of these best describes Arnold's reaction to his father?

A He was unhappy because his father didn't praise him.

B He was joyful that his father supported and encouraged him.

C He was angry that his father didn't come to his competitions.

D He was amused to learn that his father liked bodybuilding too.

6 When did Arnold win first place in the Mr. Universe Competition?

F in 1966

G when he was 18 years old

H when he was 20 years old

J before he joined the army

7 What did Arnold do once when the gym was closed?

A He went home.

B He waited outside.

C He broke in to train.

D He went to another gym.

8 Where was Arnold born?

F Germany

G France

H Austria

J Belgium

Check your answers on page 90.

Lesson 10 Character Aspects

Character aspects are personal traits or inner qualities of a person. Being able to identify the character aspects of the people you read about helps you to understand what causes them to act or behave in a certain way.

Example **Read this paragraph. How does Carlos feel about this homeless family?** _____

> Carlos Ramirez started the Goodwill Lodge Homeless Shelter in 1987. He got the idea one day when he was stopped on the sidewalk by a woman asking for money. He had seen homeless people on the street before, but there was something different about this woman. From behind her long, torn coat peered the sad eyes of a young child. Carlos thought of his son at home—safe, warm, and well-fed. Would he walk away if this were his own child?

Did you write that Carlos felt compassion and concern for the homeless family? The paragraph tells you that the woman's child reminded Carlos of his son. He asked himself if he would walk away if his own child was cold and hungry. Carlos was so deeply moved by this experience that he opened a homeless shelter to help make a difference.

To understand a person's inner qualities and inner drives:
- Look at his or her words, behaviors, and actions.
- Pay attention to how his or her feelings are described.
- Notice the events she or he is involved in.

Test Example

Read this paragraph. Answer the question by circling the letter of the best answer.

> There were more than forty children and adults living at the Goodwill Lodge during the first month that it opened. Carlos quickly learned the names of all the people. He spent time taking care of children while their parents went to look for work. He liked listening to the stories that people told about their lives. Carlos was glad that they finally had a place to stay and feel safe.

TABE Strategy

As you read, circle "feeling words" such as *proud*, *angry*, *sad*, *joyous*, and *thankful*.

1 In this paragraph, how can Carlos's feelings toward the people living at the homeless shelter be described?

A He was tired of listening to their stories.

B He was disappointed that they didn't have jobs.

C He was happy that they had a place to sleep and eat.

D He was frustrated because it was hard to learn more than forty names.

1 C The last sentence said that Carlos "was glad" that the people living at the shelter had a place to stay. Option A is incorrect because it said that he *liked* listening to their stories. Option B is incorrect because the paragraph didn't mention that Carlos was upset or disappointed. Option D is incorrect because learning their names came *quickly* to Carlos.

Practice

Read the letter that a woman sent to the homeless shelter. Answer the questions by circling the letter of the best answer.

Dear Carlos,

My name is Linda Conners. You might remember me. You used to joke around with me while I stayed at the Goodwill Lodge.

I lost my job at the fish factory about a year ago. I couldn't afford to pay my rent. So, I sold all my furniture and packed up whatever I could fit in my car. There were many cold nights that I spent huddled in the backseat hoping that no one would notice me. It was one of the scariest times in my life.

Then I heard about your shelter. I stayed at the Goodwill Lodge for six weeks. Finally I found a new job as a waitress at a nearby seafood restaurant. Soon I had enough money to pay for the first month's rent on a one-bedroom apartment. I was happy to get back on my feet again.

Thank you for having the vision to open the Goodwill Lodge Homeless Shelter. The kindness that you showed me will never be forgotten.

Thankfully yours,
Linda Conners

1 From reading the letter, you could say that Carlos and Linda both

A like to laugh

B like to eat fish

C wanted to get jobs

D have trouble sleeping

2 Which of these is probably true about Linda?

F She sold her furniture because she wanted a new bedroom set.

G She could joke around only when her life was going smoothly.

H She turned to the shelter because she didn't want to keep sleeping in her car.

J She went to the shelter because she was ill.

3 In the letter, how can Linda's feelings toward the Goodwill Lodge be described?

A She is relieved that the Goodwill Lodge is no longer open.

B She is afraid of the people who stay at the Goodwill Lodge.

C She is disappointed that she couldn't stay at the Goodwill Lodge longer.

D She is grateful that the Goodwill Lodge was there when she needed a place to stay.

Check your answers on pages 90–91.

The main idea is the general topic of a passage. When you read, it is important to know the basic meaning of what you are reading. The TABE will ask you to identify the main idea of short excerpts or passages.

Example   Read the paragraph. What is it mostly about?_____

_____

> In 1943, the aqua-lung was invented. The aqua-lung is carried on a scuba diver's back. It allows a diver to breathe enough air to stay underwater for several hours. Before the invention of the aqua-lung, divers had to breathe using long air hoses that reached the water's surface.

The first sentence of this paragraph tells what the paragraph is about. It is called a *topic sentence*. A topic sentence "sums up" or gives a short summary of a paragraph's main idea. Often the topic sentence is the first or the last sentence of a paragraph.

Did you write that the paragraph is about the invention of the aqua-lung? The paragraph explains what an aqua-lung is and what it does.

Test Example

Read this paragraph. Answer the question by circling the letter of the best answer.

> Masks, fins, and snorkels are three basic but important pieces of equipment that a diver needs. To see clearly underwater, divers use a mask. They use fins to move quickly through the water. To be able to swim face-down, a diver needs a snorkel. This makes swimming much easier than lifting the head up to breathe. Before buying any other scuba equipment, a diver should first purchase a good mask, snorkel, and fins.

1   Which of these is the best title for this excerpt?

  A   "Diving in the Caribbean"

  B   "How to Use a Snorkel"

  C   "Learning to Scuba Dive"

  D   "Basic Diving Equipment"

TABE Strategy

To get the main idea of a passage, try underlining the first and last sentence of every paragraph. Reread them in order. This will provide you with a short summary of the passage.

1   D   The excerpt is about the three basic pieces of equipment needed to scuba dive: a mask, fins, and a snorkel. The paragraph doesn't mention *where* to dive (option A). The paragraph doesn't go into detail about *how to use* the equipment (option B). The paragraph doesn't tell *how* to scuba dive (option C).

This passage is about a famous underwater explorer. Read the passage and answer the questions by circling the letter of the best answer.

Jacques Cousteau was born in France in 1910. Ever since he was a child, Jacques loved the water. He knew that he always wanted to be near the ocean.

In 1933 Cousteau joined the French Navy. It was during his service that he began his underwater explorations. In 1937 Cousteau married Simone Melchoir, and they had two sons. Two years after their marriage, Cousteau fought for the French in World War II. During the war, he still found time to continue his underwater work. In 1943, he helped invent the aqua-lung, which allowed a diver to stay underwater for several hours. The aqua-lung was used to locate and remove underwater enemy mines.

In 1951 Cousteau bought a ship to further his explorations. He named it *Calypso*. To pay for his trips on *Calypso*, he made underwater films and wrote many books about ocean life. He also created a TV show called *The Undersea World of Jacques Cousteau*. This popular show was on television for about nine years.

In 1974 Jacques established the Cousteau Society. It worked to help people understand and protect the water systems of the planet. Cousteau was awarded the Presidential Medal of Freedom in 1985. In 1989 the French honored Cousteau with membership in the French Academy. Jacques Cousteau died in 1997. He will always be remembered for being a great inventor and explorer who helped educate the world about ocean life.

1 What is this passage mostly about?

A a popular TV show about sea animals

B a famous inventor and underwater explorer

C how underwater mines were used in World War II

D a group that helps to educate people about ocean life

2 Which of these is the best title for the excerpt?

F "The Story of *Calypso*"

G "My Life as an Inventor"

H "Famous French Explorers"

J "The Life of Jacques Cousteau"

3 Which of these best tells about Jacques Cousteau's life?

A He spent his life helping others learn about ocean life.

B He fought bravely in World War II and was a war hero.

C He taught French scuba divers how to use the aqua-lung.

D He was a devoted family man who had a wife and two sons.

4 When was the Cousteau Society formed?

F 1910

G 1933

H 1974

J 1997

Check your answers on page 91.

Lesson 12 | Summary and Paraphrase

A summary is a brief report that covers the main points. Being able to sum up what you have read in one or two concise sentences is useful when writing a short report. It is also a useful verbal skill when you want to briefly tell others the main idea of an article or a story. On the TABE you will be asked to choose a summary that rewords the main points of a passage.

Example **Read the paragraph. Write a one-sentence summary of the main points.**

Dogs play an important role in search and rescue. They are able to locate missing people even when they are hidden from view. A search dog's main tool is its keen sense of smell. Wherever a person goes, he or she leaves behind a scent. A trained dog can follow a particular scent and lead a team of rescuers on the right trail. Because of this ability, dogs are often able to reduce search time, thereby increasing the chances that a person will be found.

The summary is: Search dogs use their keen sense of smell to find missing people.
- A summary is the general idea of a passage.
- A summary is not just a fact taken from the passage.
- A summary usually includes a subject, an action, and an outcome.

Subject	Action	Outcome
search dogs	follow scents	find missing people

Test Example

Read the paragraph. Answer the question by circling the letter of the best answer.

King is a three-year-old golden retriever. He has been trained to search for missing people. On Monday afternoon, King helped to locate a lost hiker. The hiker was last seen leaving for a weekend hiking trip in Green Mountain National Park. King was given a sample of the hiker's clothing to sniff. He used the scent to lead rescuers down a three-mile trail. The hiker was found lying near a stream. He had a broken leg that he got when he fell off a rocky ledge.

TABE Strategy

As you read the passage, underline the *subject, action,* and *outcome*. Then choose a summary that includes all three.

1 Which of these is a statement about King that a reporter would probably tell on the evening news?

A King has gone through a training program.

B King likes to hike in Green Mountain National Park.

C King, a search dog, led rescuers to a missing hiker in Green Mountain National Park.

D King's sense of smell helps him find missing people.

1 C This summary includes the *subject*: King; the *action*: leading rescuers; and the *outcome*: finding the missing hiker. Options A and D are facts from the paragraph, but they don't sum up the event. The statement in option B is not accurate. The paragraph says that King located a hiker, not that King likes to hike.

Practice

Read the passage. Answer the questions by circling the letter of the best answer.

The list of responsibilities of an animal control worker is long. Animal control workers drive trucks to look for stray animals. When stray animals are captured, workers take them to an animal shelter. At the shelter, workers check animals for tags. They fill out reports about where they found the animals and write descriptions of them. They use the reports to help find a pet's owners.

The invention of the pet microchip has helped to make the job of an animal control worker much easier. This special computer chip carries the pet's personal identification number. Using a microchip reader, the worker can access a database that has the owner's name, address, and telephone number. The chip can't be lost or damaged, and it lasts for an animal's lifetime.

Pets that have microchips get reunited with their owners much faster than pets that do not. Pets that have chips spend less time in animal shelters. Because of pet microchips, animal control workers can spend more time catching stray animals and less time filling out paperwork.

1 Which of these best summarizes the passage?

A Animal control workers are hard to find because of all their responsibilities.

B Pet microchips help animal control workers find a pet's owners without having to write long reports.

C Pet microchips help owners keep their pets safe.

D Pet microchips are small, but they contain important information.

2 Which of these best describes how the pet microchip makes it easier to reunite lost pets with their owners?

F Animal control workers don't need to write long reports.

G The chip can't be lost or damaged and it lasts for an animal's lifetime.

H The microchips have an identification number that allows access to information about pet owners.

J Animal control workers have more time to do their jobs.

3 Which of these best describes the duties and responsibilities of an animal control worker?

A Animal control workers enter information about a pet's owners into a computer database.

B Animal control workers feed and take care of animals.

C Animal control workers monitor the health of the shelter's animals.

D Animal control workers capture stray animals, bring them to a shelter, and try to locate pet owners.

Check your answers on page 91.

Cause and Effect

The terms *cause* and *effect* are related. A *cause* is a *reason* that leads to an effect. An *effect* is what happens as a *result* of the cause. For example, a hole in the roof could be the cause for water dripping into a house. Being aware of cause-effect relationships helps one better understand why events happen.

Example **Read the paragraph. How did the 1950s medical studies linking smoking and lung cancer affect the cigarette market?** _____

> Before the 1950s people smoked unfiltered cigarettes. There was no proof that cigarettes were harmful. Cigarette companies spent a lot of money trying to make people believe that cigarettes were fine. But that all changed with the release of the first medical studies linking smoking and lung cancer. One response to these studies was the filter-tip cigarette. The filter was supposed to screen out tar and nicotine, thereby making cigarettes "safer."

The effect was that cigarette companies starting selling filter-tip cigarettes. The paragraph explains that medical studies showed that cigarettes were linked to cancer. Companies added filters to make cigarettes "safer" so people would keep buying them.

Test Example

Read the paragraph. Answer the question by circling the letter of the best answer.

> The problem with filtered cigarettes is that they don't really help smokers take in less nicotine. They might filter out some of the nicotine, but a smoker's body will crave more. It's a physical addiction. A smoker will smoke as many cigarettes as it takes to get the amount of nicotine the body is used to receiving.

TABE Strategy

Highlight the key words *how* or *why* in TABE questions. Then ask yourself if each answer choice is true, accurate, and answers the exact question.

1   Which of these best explains why a smoker may inhale twice as many filtered cigarettes as unfiltered ones?

   A   Filtered cigarettes help smokers crave less nicotine.

   B   Filtered cigarettes taste better than unfiltered cigarettes.

   C   Unfiltered cigarettes are more addictive.

   D   More filtered cigarettes need to be smoked to get the amount of nicotine that a smoker's body is used to receiving.

1   D A person may smoke more filtered cigarettes to get enough nicotine. Filtered cigarettes do not help smokers crave less nicotine (option A). The paragraph doesn't mention the taste of cigarettes (option B). Option C is not supported by the paragraph.

Read the passage. Answer the questions by circling the letter of the best answer.

The larynx is the voice box. Cancer can strike in many different parts of the voice box. The typical person who develops throat cancer has a history of smoking.

The treatment of throat cancer depends on how large the tumor is and its location in the voice box. Small cancers can be treated with radiation, laser surgery, or by removing a small part of the voice box. Large tumors often require removal of the entire voice box, as well as radiation.

People who have their entire voice box removed can still communicate by using a special device to help them speak. When the person talks, a mechanical voice is activated.

Cancer of the throat is curable if it is caught early. If you have a lump in your neck that won't go away, you should see a doctor. The best way to prevent this kind of cancer is to quit smoking. Tobacco causes serious damage to the throat. Over time the damage can turn into cancer. If it is not treated, it can spread to other parts of the body and become life-threatening.

1 Which of these best explains why a person might have his or her voice box removed?

A He or she has a history of smoking.

B He or she has a lump on the neck.

C He or she has a large, cancerous tumor on the larynx.

D He or she can no longer communicate with the voice box.

2 How can a person communicate without a voice box?

F He or she can get a new voice box.

G He or she can use a special device that helps with speech.

H He or she can use a computer that has a mechanical voice.

J He or she can get laser surgery to remove cancer from the voice box.

3 According to the passage, how might a lump on a person's neck affect a person's health?

A It could be cancerous.

B It might cause a person to stop breathing.

C It could travel into a person's stomach.

D It could make speaking very difficult.

4 Which of these is the best reason to quit smoking?

F Over time tobacco damage can turn into cancer.

G Cancer can strike in many different parts of the voice box.

H Tobacco can cause serious damage to the throat.

J Smoking is not good for your vocal cords or larynx.

Check your answers on page 91.

Lesson 14   Compare and Contrast

Authors often use descriptive language to compare or contrast feelings, people, places, events, and things. Thinking about how an author compares and contrasts will help you to better understand an author's message. It will also help you to get more pleasure and meaning out of what you read. To identify when an author compares and contrasts, look for context clues that describe actions and feelings. Pay attention to what characters say and how they act.

Example   Read the paragraph. How have Jennifer's feelings about moving changed since speaking with her Uncle Diego? _____

> Jennifer started to question whether or not she should move to Florida. Would she be able to find a good job right away? How would she support her son, Tomas, in the meantime? Jennifer paced around the room until she got a phone call from her uncle Diego in Miami. Jennifer let out a long sigh when she heard the good news. Her uncle wanted her to work at his restaurant.

Context clues about Jennifer's feelings

Jennifer's feelings changed from worried to relieved. At first, Jennifer "paced around the room" because she was worried about not being able to support her son. When her uncle offered her a job, Jennifer "let out a long sigh" because she felt relieved.

Test Example

Read the paragraph. Answer the question by circling the letter of the best answer.

> As the holiday season came nearer, Jennifer began to long for familiar traditions. She started to daydream about her old neighborhood in Puerto Rico. She remembered the excitement that surrounded this time of year. Tomas seemed to share Jennifer's homesickness. He pointed to his uncle's guitar and pleaded, "Mama, can we please have a party like we used to in Puerto Rico?"

TABE Strategy

As you read TABE passages, circle the context words that describe actions or feelings.

1   Right before the holiday season, Jennifer and Tomas both

     A   felt sick and wanted to rest

     B   wanted to go to a guitar concert

     C   missed the holiday traditions in Puerto Rico

     D   wanted to daydream about Puerto Rico

1   **C**   Jennifer "daydreamed" about and "longed for" holiday traditions. Tomas did too. We know this because he "pleaded" for a holiday party. They weren't sick (option A); they were homesick. They didn't want to go to a guitar concert (option B). They didn't want to daydream about Puerto Rico (option D); they wanted to be there.

Read the passage. Answer the questions by circling the letter of the best answer.

Jennifer sat down on the stoop to talk with her uncle Diego about how things were going. "Everything is working out better than I ever could have imagined." Still, as she said this, Jennifer's mouth turned down at the corners.

"Then why do you look so sad?" asked Diego.

She began to explain. "The holiday season makes me think of Puerto Rico. One of my favorite times during the holidays is when friends gather in the evening to go from one house to the next, singing traditional songs."

"Yes!" exclaimed Diego. "I remember. In the neighborhood I grew up in, we went from house to house with musical instruments. The best part," Diego went on, "was when we were invited in for food, drinks, and dancing.

"But Jennifer, we stick to traditions here. This neighborhood has its own version of your favorite tradition. We may not sing all the songs that you are used to, but it's still a wonderful party. The singing and dancing usually last until the next morning."

An overwhelming sense of peace swept over Jennifer. She realized that didn't have to miss home anymore. Finally she felt as if she were already at home.

1 By the end of the story, how have Jennifer's feelings changed?

A from furious to pleased

B from indifferent to curious

C from proud to embarrassed

D from homesick to comforted

2 From reading the passage, you could say that both Jennifer and Diego

F miss Puerto Rico and wish to return for the holidays

G have fond memories of growing up with the same holiday tradition

H hope to go from house to house to ask neighbors to join a singing group

J know a lot about Puerto Rican history

3 Which of these best summarizes the passage?

A A woman finds a way to go home for the holidays.

B A woman realizes that you can feel at home away from home.

C A woman works hard and saves money.

D A woman finds a way to keep the spirit of her heritage alive.

4 Which of these best explains why Jennifer was homesick?

F She liked singing traditional songs.

G The holiday parties lasted until the morning.

H She didn't like her new home.

J She missed taking part in holiday traditions.

Check your answers on pages 91–92.

A conclusion is what you can determine or infer from given information. Because authors sometimes hint at subtle meanings, readers must piece together information to make conclusions. Understanding the full meaning of an author's message helps you to become more engaged in what you read.

Example **Read the paragraph. How do salamanders breathe?** _____

> Salamanders live in streams, rivers, ponds, lakes, and moist woodlands. Most salamanders breathe by using gills, just like fish, or by using lungs, just like humans. Some salamanders don't have lungs or gills, but absorb oxygen from water through their skin.

Salamanders breathe using lungs, gills, or through their skin. This can be concluded from the information in the paragraph.

From the Given Information
• The paragraph states that most salamanders breathe with gills or lungs.
• The paragraph states that some salamanders absorb oxygen through their skin.
• "Absorbing oxygen" means the same as breathing.

You Can Make This Conclusion
• Salamanders breathe using lungs, gills, or through their skin.

Test Example

Read the paragraph. Answer the question by circling the letter of the best answer.

> Salamanders are amazing creatures. They swim like eels, using muscles to propel themselves through the water. They can also walk on land by moving one leg at a time. Salamanders are true survivors. They have the ability to shed their tails and grow them back, as well as regrow other damaged parts of their bodies.

Hint

Carefully put together the facts when making conclusions.

1 What does "salamanders are true survivors" mean?

  A Salamanders can remain alive without skin.

  B Salamanders can travel on land and in water.

  C Salamanders can glide through the water and escape from eels.

  D Salamanders can regrow an injured body part.

---

1 **D** "Surviving" means staying alive. Their ability to regrow body parts would help them survive if a body part was hurt. Option A is not mentioned. Being able to travel on land and in water (option B) is not a survival skill. Salamanders can glide like eels, not escape from them (option C).

Read the article. Answer the questions by circling the letter of the best answer.

Salamander Crossing

A new traffic sign has been put up on Henry Street. It's different than any sign you've seen before. It's a sign for a "salamander crossing." The sign marks new salamander-crossing tunnels that have been installed under Henry Street.

For most of the year, salamanders live in a large park on Henry Street. Every spring the salamanders cross Henry Street to get to a pond where they mate and lay their eggs. The journey happens mostly at night, which makes it difficult for drivers to see salamanders crossing the road.

Local residents expressed their relief over the completion of the project. One homeowner said, "I was tired of seeing the little critters getting squashed every spring by careless drivers."

The two tunnels, about twenty feet apart, were built at the salamanders' regular crossing site. Short fences were put up to guide migrating salamanders into the tunnels. Each tunnel has a slot in the top to let in light and to provide the wet conditions that the salamanders need. People who are interested in watching the salamanders migrate can park at the nearby train station.

1 The purpose of the "salamander crossing" is to

A make the road wider for pedestrians, cyclists, and salamanders

B give salamanders a safe way to cross the road and get to the pond

C warn drivers to slow down for the tunnel

D give residents a pathway to the pond to see the salamanders mate

2 Which of these probably happened before the salamander crossing was built?

F Salamanders found a different route to get to the pond.

G Salamanders laid their eggs in puddles by the side of the road.

H Salamanders were crossing the street and getting run over by cars.

J Police officers stopped traffic for the salamanders to cross the road.

3 Why was a sign put up?

A to mark the location where people can watch the migration

B to warn drivers to slow down for salamanders crossing the street

C to mark the location of the pond where the salamanders lay their eggs

D to warn drivers to slow down for children

4 Which of these details from the article best shows how residents feel about the salamander crossing?

F Slots were put on the tunnels to let light and moisture in.

G Residents can park at the train station to watch the migration.

H One resident is relieved the salamanders are not getting squashed.

J The two tunnels are built twenty feet apart.

Check your answers on page 92.

Supporting evidence is information that backs up a statement. It is important to have evidence that supports your position or statement. As a result, what you say is more believable. The TABE will ask you to choose a statement that has plenty of supporting evidence to back it up.

Example **Read the paragraph. Find two facts from the paragraph to support this statement: Annie Oakley was good at shooting a gun.**

Fact 1: _____

Fact 2: _____

As a child, Annie Oakley learned to shoot wild animals for food. Her career as a sharpshooter started at age 17 when she beat the famous gunslinger Frank E. Butler at a competition in Cincinnati, Ohio. The two eventually married and performed with the Buffalo Bill Show for 17 years.

Fact 1: Annie shot wild animals for food. Fact 2: She beat a famous gunslinger during a shooting contest. These two facts from the paragraph can be used to back up, or support, the statement "Annie Oakley was good at shooting a gun."

Test Example

Read the paragraph. Answer the question by circling the letter of the best answer.

The American West produced many exciting heroes and legends, but none were as entertaining as Annie Oakley. One time she shot a cigarette from the hand of a prince. At thirty paces she could slice a playing card in half. It was said that she could even "scramble" eggs in midair.

TABE Strategy

Read each answer choice. Cross off the answer choices that are not supported by facts from the passage.

1 Which of these statements is best supported by the paragraph?

A Annie Oakley was a legendary sharpshooter.

B Becoming a good shooter requires concentration.

C The most famous marksmen were good at cooking.

D Annie Oakley shot accurately only from a short distance.

1 **A** Option A is correct because the first sentence describes Annie as a legend of the American West. The paragraph doesn't say that Annie had to concentrate to shoot accurately (option B). It doesn't mention cooking (option C) or say anything about shooting from short distances (option D).

Read the passage. Answer the questions by circling the letter of the best answer.

By the 1930s, tennis had become a popular American sport. However, at that time tennis was dominated mostly by white athletes. Becoming a famous tennis player was still only a dream to African American children.

Althea Gibson changed all that. She became the first African American woman to win a major singles tennis tournament. She was able to show the world that tennis was ready for a change.

Althea was born on a cotton farm in South Carolina, where her parents were sharecroppers. She later moved to Harlem, New York, where she spent most of her childhood. She had trouble in school and often ran away from home.

Developing an interest in tennis was hard because Althea was banned from most public courts because she was African American. She finally learned to play in a public program that brought tennis to children in poor neighborhoods. Her talent and interest in the game helped her win several local tournaments. She won the New York state championship six times from 1944–1950. In 1957, Althea Gibson became the first black player to win at Wimbledon and was named the Associated Press Female Athlete of the year.

1 Which of these facts best supports the statement, *You can rise to the top with talent and determination?*

A Althea got into trouble at school, but she still graduated.

B Although banned from public courts, Althea still became a great tennis player.

C Even though Althea was born on a farm, she was interested in tennis.

D Even though she was poor, Althea still wanted to play.

2 Which of these statements is best supported by the passage?

F The most famous athletes are tennis players.

G Becoming a tennis player requires access to good coaches.

H A sport may not recognize an athlete right away based on skill alone.

J The talent of a woman is not always recognized in male-dominated sports.

3 By the end of the story, how had Althea's tennis career changed?

A from banned to ignored

B from celebrated to acknowledged

C from acknowledged to ignored

D from banned to celebrated

Check your answers on page 92.

Read the passage. Answer the questions by circling the letter of the best answer.

For years, my father, Manuel Rivera, regularly traveled from town to town. Everything he owned had to be small enough to fit in an oversized army backpack. He worked as a migrant worker. Home was wherever the next harvest was. Moving around to different places suited my father just fine until he met my mother.

"I was used to moving around. It was the life that my parents had and that I followed. Picking fruits and vegetables was what I knew best," he explained. "Then I met your mother and that all changed. I realized that I did not want that kind of life for my children. My dream became to have a home so my own family could have a better life," he told me.

My mother, Helena Garcia, was born in Mexico. When her mother died, Helena and her father moved to the United States. Helena surprised her family when she told them she wanted to become a nurse. She became the first in her family to go to college. She took out a student loan and went to a local community college. During the summers, she picked strawberries to help pay for tuition. That was where she met my father. They got married but owning a home of their own seemed out of reach. Thankfully, an organization called Habitat for Humanity opened a door that may not have opened otherwise. "Habitat helped us to afford a good home where we could raise a family and teach our children the value of education," said my parents.

Using volunteer labor and donated materials, the non-profit group Habitat for Humanity built a simple but sturdy house for us. My parents even helped the volunteers build it. When it was done, my mother got a job in nursing and my father worked at a grocery store. It was the first time in his life that he could work around fruits and vegetables without having to move!

1 Which of these is the best title for the passage?

A "The Story of My Life"

B "Life as a Migrant Worker"

C "How Our Home Came to Be"

D "Fruit and Vegetable Farming"

2 Habitat for Humanity probably acquired its name because

F it provides temporary shelter to migrant workers

G it provides affordable homes to low-income families

H it gives opportunities for volunteer work

J it teaches families how to grow their own fruits and vegetables

3 Which of these best explains why the author's father stopped picking fruits and vegetables?

A He lost his job.

B He got a new job in a grocery store.

C He wanted to learn how to build houses.

D He didn't want his family to have to move around.

4 From the passage, you can tell that the author's mother wants

F her children to go to school

G to own her own strawberry farm

H to move back in with her parents

J her husband to pay for her college tuition

5 Which of these best summarizes the last two paragraphs of the passage?

A Habitat for Humanity provided one town with low-cost housing.

B A migrant worker earns a college degree and gets a better paying job.

C Habitat for Humanity helped one family live the dream of having a permanent home.

D A man and a woman get married and raise children in Mexico.

6 By the end of the excerpt, how did the father's feelings change about living the life of a migrant worker?

F from bored to enthusiastic

G from content to dissatisfied

H from appreciative to resentful

J from disenchanted to fulfilled

7 Which of these statements is best supported by the passage?

A Habitat for Humanity builds expensive houses.

B Migrant work is a good way to save money to buy a house.

C The author's mother was used to living in a comfortable home.

D The author's father felt at home wherever he was working.

8 What does the author mean when he says of his father, "It was the first time in his life that he could work around fruits and vegetables without having to move!"?

F This was his father's first job that didn't have to do with food.

G His father wanted to work in a grocery store because he liked traveling.

H His father's new job still involved produce, but it did not require traveling.

J His father's new job required moving fruits and vegetables, not picking them.

9 Which of these is probably true of Manuel Rivera?

A He considers family first.

B He prefers traveling to staying in one place.

C He is used to sleeping on floors.

D He enjoys carpentry.

10 From the passage, you can tell that the author and his parents

F don't know their family history

G appreciate what Habitat for Humanity did for them

H want to go back to being migrant workers

J live in a fancy new house

Check your answers on pages 92–93.

Lesson 17 Fact and Opinion

On the TABE you will have to decide whether a statement in a passage is a fact or an opinion. Facts are based on true information. Opinions are personal views or judgments.

Example **Read the two sentences. Can you tell which one is a fact and which one is**

an opinion? Fact: _____. Opinion: _____.

Sentence 1 Baxter State Park is located in Maine.
Sentence 2 It is one of the most beautiful wilderness areas in the Northeast.

Sentence 1 is a fact and Sentence 2 is an opinion. The location of Baxter State Park is a fact. However, not everyone might agree that Baxter State Park is one of the most beautiful wilderness areas in the Northeast. That is a personal opinion.

When an opinion is expressed, it usually includes descriptive judgment words. Some examples of descriptive judgment words are in the chart.

Descriptive Judgment Words	
Positive	**Negative**
beautiful	ugly
perfect	flawed
smart	dumb
wonderful	terrible
best	worst

Test Example

Read the paragraph. Answer the question by circling the letter of the best answer.

Baxter State Park is an area that has a history of logging. The first logging was for pine; then spruce; then pulpwood. Baxter was logged from the mid-1800s until 1965. Then logging rights expired and the area was turned into a state-protected preserve. Baxter State Park should be reopened to commercial logging. Keeping the woods from being harvested is a terrible waste of good lumber.

TABE Strategy

As you read TABE passages, highlight descriptive judgment words that may indicate an opinion.

1 Which of these is an opinion?

A The area was logged until 1965.

B The first logging was for pine.

C Keeping the woods from being harvested is a terrible waste of good lumber.

D The logging rights ended and the area was turned into a state park.

1 C The words "terrible waste" indicate an opinion or a personal view of the author. Not everyone would agree. Because option A is a date, it is factual. Option B describes the actual types of wood that were harvested. Option D is a historical statement about how it became a state park.

Read the letter. Answer the questions by circling the letter of the best answer.

Dear Friends and Neighbors:

I am outraged that our state leaders are considering selling commercial logging rights in Baxter State Park. The park is one of Maine's most treasured areas. It was donated by Percival P. Baxter to preserve the area in its natural state. It is an important piece of Maine's natural history that should not be spoiled for profit.

Baxter is home to numerous ponds, lakes, streams, waterfalls, and bogs. This all combines to create a magnificent landscape. People from all over New England go hiking and camping in Baxter. The fall foliage in Baxter is spectacular. Taking down the trees would ruin much of the natural beauty.

Many unique plants and wildlife reside within the park. Removing trees would disturb the delicate balance of nature that the animals depend on for their survival.

Many of Maine's forests are under attack from over-harvesting and new development. Let's work together to protect the woods of Baxter from this fate. Baxter State Park should remain in its natural state and continue to be a sanctuary for all to enjoy.

A Concerned Resident of Maine

1 Which of these is an <u>opinion</u> expressed in the letter?

A The fall foliage here is spectacular.

B Baxter is home to numerous ponds.

C Many unique plants and wildlife reside within the park.

D People from all over New England go hiking and camping in Baxter.

2 Which of these sentences from the letter expresses a <u>fact</u>?

F The park is one of Maine's most treasured areas.

G This all combines to create a magnificent landscape.

H Let's work together to protect the woods of Baxter from this fate.

J It was donated by Percival P. Baxter.

3 Which of these is an <u>opinion</u>?

A Baxter State Park is in Maine.

B Ponds can be used for fishing.

C Taking down trees would ruin the natural beauty.

D Baxter State Park has hiking trails.

4 Which of these sentences expresses a <u>fact</u>?

F The park is a wonderful gift that we should protect.

G It is an important piece of Maine's natural history.

H Baxter State Park should remain in its natural state.

J The animals that live in the park include moose, deer, bears, and otters.

Check your answers on page 93.

Lesson 18 Predict Outcomes

Some TABE questions will ask you to read a sentence or paragraph and decide what will happen next, or predict outcomes. Understanding what we read, prior knowledge, and experience help us predict outcomes—when we read and in everyday life. A parent, for example, might predict that a child will feel ill if he or she eats too many cookies.

Example **Read the paragraph. Then use what you learn and know to predict what**

will happen next. _____

Natalie grinned as she laced her new shoes; they fit perfectly. Slipping them over athletic socks, she began stretching. Finishing, she clipped on her pedometer and water bottle. She grabbed her house keys and hurried out the door.

Did you predict that Natalie was going to run, jog, or walk? You probably noticed word clues in the passage: *athletic, stretching,* and *pedometer.* In addition, you may have known that people often carry water bottles when they exercise.

Test Example

Read the paragraph. As you read, look for word clues that help you predict the outcome of the paragraph. Answer the question by circling the letter of the best answer.

An hour later, a damp, flushed Natalie placed both hands on the living room wall and began her series of stretches. Fifteen minutes later, Natalie moved into the kitchen, where she removed fresh pasta and marinara sauce from the refrigerator. Placing a pan of water on the stove to boil, she sat at the table with a large glass of cold water.

Hint

A logical prediction must be supported by passage details.

1 What outcome likely will result from Natalie's actions?
   A She will visit a friend.
   B She will go to work.
   C She will attend a party.
   D She will eat a meal.

1 **D** Details such as pasta, marinara sauce, and the pan of water on the stove hint that Natalie is preparing a meal. In addition, previous knowledge and experience may have told you that people are hungry after they exercise. Although the other choices are possible, no clue words in the paragraph indicate that Natalie will visit a friend (option A), go to work (option B), or attend a party (option C).

Read each paragraph. Using what you read and what you already know, answer numbers 1 through 3 by circling the letter of the best answer.

1

Today, the word *marathon* is used to indicate a long-distance race or endurance contest. The name comes from a legend about a Greek soldier who ran nonstop more than 25 miles to Athens to announce the defeat of the Persians at the Battle of Marathon.

What most likely happened next?

A The runner ran back to Marathon nonstop to join the celebration.

B The runner collapsed in exhaustion after making his announcement.

C The runner joined the Persian Army.

D The runner forgot to deliver the message.

2

In the late nineteenth century, Frenchmen Michel Bréal and Pierre de Coubertin wanted to create a marathon race to honor the Greek legend. The Greek people supported the idea and staged a selection race in Athens. The winner, Charilaos Vasilakos, finished the marathon in 3 hours 18 minutes. People were thrilled at the idea of more marathon races and other contests of athletic skill, strength, and endurance.

The creation of which of the following is the most likely outcome of the events in the paragraph?

F the Cannes Film Festival

G the Academy Awards

H the Super Bowl

J the Olympic Games

3

Rivalry between ancient cities extended to marathons and other athletic contests. The success of athletes brought honor to their communities. Astylos of Kroton ran in three competitions from 488 B.C. to 480 B.C. In the first, he ran for the city of Kroton. When he won, the people of Kroton proudly honored him with statues. In the next two Olympiads, he ran and won as a citizen of Syracuse.

Based on the paragraph, it is likely that

A Astylos moved back to Kroton

B the people of Syracuse denied Astylos citizenship

C the people of Kroton destroyed Astylos's statues

D the cities of Kroton and Syracuse merged

Check your answers on page 93.

Lesson 19 | Apply Passage Elements

Applying information is the same as putting it to specific or practical use. For example, when you are reading a history article, you may be able to apply the information to current events. Or, you may be able to extend the lesson or moral of a story about someone else to your own daily life.

Example **Read the paragraph. What advice would Devon give to friends who are thinking about staying outside during a thunderstorm?** _____

> Devon was up on a ladder fixing a rain gutter when the storm started. He wondered if he should go inside when he heard a loud bang of thunder. He continued to work because he was almost done. That was when the lightning hit. The next thing he knew, Devon was lying on the ground, feeling very dizzy. Luckily he was not too hurt to get up and go into the house to call an ambulance.

Devon would probably advise his friends to go indoors during a thunderstorm. He might tell his friends his story and warn them to stay inside so the same thing does not happen to them.

Test Example

Read the paragraph. Answer the question by circling the letter of the best answer.

> At the hospital, a doctor examined Devon. The doctor explained to Devon that lightning must have hit the ladder he was on. Devon felt lucky to be alive. He decided to spend the rest of the weekend with his children instead of working on the house as he had planned.

TABE Strategy

As you read the TABE passage, identify and underline or write down the lesson or the moral.

1   With which of these statements would Devon most likely agree?

   A   A wooden ladder is better than a metal one.

   B   It is important to repair things before they break.

   C   Working on a ladder is dangerous.

   D   Spending time with family is more important than getting the job done.

1   **D**   Devon said that he felt "lucky to be alive." That was what made him realize that spending time with his family is more important to him than working on the house. The paragraph didn't mention what kind of ladder Devon was working on (option A). At the end of the paragraph, he is no longer interested in fixing things on the house (option B). The danger was the lightning, not the ladder (option C).

Read the passage. Answer the questions by circling the letter of the best answer.

It was noisy inside the dam, but Trisha could still hear the tour guide. "Water from the lake passes through large, fanlike machines called turbines," he shouted. "The water turns those giant fans and creates electricity."

Trisha marveled at all the machinery. Everything was made out of concrete and metal. She walked over to one of the turbines. It was as tall as a house and made of steel. "I'd sure like to climb that thing," she said out loud. "I bet I could make it to the top."

Just then, the tour guide tapped her on the shoulder. "Be careful around that turbine! It's powerful and can be dangerous." The tour guide continued. "Hydro-power is currently the world's largest renewable source of electricity. It accounts for about fifteen percent of the world's electricity and is an inexpensive and clean source of power. The electricity created by this dam lights communities many miles away!"

For a moment, Trisha thought of her life without electricity. "Without electricity, I couldn't watch TV." Her mind raced on. "I couldn't listen to music because the stereo wouldn't work. I couldn't play my new computer game because the computer wouldn't even turn on."

When Trisha's group walked outside again, Trisha looked up at the top of the dam way above her. "One day," she thought, "I'd like to work on a big turbine in a dam."

1 With which of these statements would the tour guide probably agree?

A Windmills are the best form of alternative energy.

B More hydro-dams should be built around the world.

C Water should not be used for anything except drinking.

D Rivers should not be dammed.

2 At the end of the excerpt, if Trisha heard someone in the next group complaining about having to go on the tour, she would most likely respond by

F talking about her career plans

G ignoring them

H explaining how valuable hydro-dams are to people

J vigorously agreeing with them

3 What advice would the tour guide probably offer to people who are interested in developing alternative forms of energy?

A Water can be used to create an endless supply of power.

B Coal- and oil-fueled power plants are inexpensive to build.

C The world has enough renewable sources of energy already.

D Consumers should be taught ways to conserve electricity.

4 From reading the passage, you can tell that Trisha

F is not interested in working in a dam

G takes having electricity for granted

H is interested in machinery

J doesn't like computer games

Check your answers on page 94.

When you generalize, you apply information to other situations. Some TABE questions will require you to think beyond what you have read. You must use the information from the passage to generalize and choose the answer that makes the most sense.

Example **Read this paragraph about polio. Should American parents Nancy and Tom get their baby vaccinated against polio? _____**

> Polio is a serious disease. There is no cure for it. Therefore, the best way to avoid the disease is prevention. The United States and many other countries are free of polio. However, because of world-wide travel, it is important for people to have immunity to the disease. This will prevent it from spreading and causing an epidemic.

Nancy and Tom *should* get their baby vaccinated against polio. The answer is not directly stated in the paragraph, but it can be generalized from the information given.

Test Example

Read the paragraph. Answer the question by circling the letter of the best answer.

> In the past, polio was common and greatly feared. It left thousands of people dependent on braces, crutches, and wheelchairs. In the 1950s, however, a vaccine against the disease was introduced.

TABE Strategy

First eliminate the answer choices that, based on what you read, don't seem likely or possible.

1 Based on the paragraph, which of these is probably true?

   A Polio affects only children.

   B Braces were used to help prevent polio.

   C Some people affected with polio cannot walk.

   D Before 1950, people were not as afraid of contracting polio.

1 C The paragraph states that many people who have had polio use braces, crutches, and wheelchairs. Therefore, polio must affect people's ability to walk. Readers cannot assume that all polio victims are children (option A). Braces are used to help people walk (option B), not to prevent polio. Option D is not correct because people were not as afraid of contracting polio *after* the introduction of the vaccine in the 1950s.

Read the passage. Answer the questions by circling the letter of the best answer.

When Europeans sailed across the Atlantic Ocean to North America, they brought many things with them. They introduced horses, cows, and oxen to the Native Americans. They also brought diseases. Smallpox was one of the most deadly diseases. It wiped out entire tribes of Native Americans.

The Europeans had already been exposed to smallpox, so they were often protected from catching the disease—or at least from dying from it. But Native Americans had no resistance to smallpox. Many of them died as a result of being exposed to it.

When the Europeans met the Native Americans, the smallpox virus passed from the Europeans' lungs into the lungs of the Native Americans. Smallpox also infected bedding and clothing. As trading began between the two groups, blankets and other goods made their way into the villages, exposing more people to the disease.

With the invention of the steamboat, more trade routes opened and goods were brought into new trading posts. This set the stage for disaster as smallpox was able to reach new victims.

It is estimated that diseases killed between 100,000 to 300,000 Native Americans in the mid-nineteenth century. Smallpox was, by far, the biggest killer. It greatly reduced the Native American population and changed their culture forever.

1 The invention of the steamboat made

A travel more difficult

B buffalo hides more expensive for buyers

C infected blankets more available to isolated tribes

D trading more confrontational between fur traders and blanket traders

2 Based on the passage, which of these is probably true?

F The Europeans were all vaccinated against smallpox.

G Smallpox is a disease that was not native to North America.

H Smallpox helped Native American culture grow and expand.

J The Atlantic Ocean prevented many diseases from being brought to America.

3 How can Native Americans living today be protected against diseases?

A They can get vaccinations.

B They can stop using blankets.

C They can wear face masks for protection.

D They can stay in America and never go to Europe.

Check your answers on page 94.

Lesson 21 Effect and Intention

On the TABE, you will answer questions about a person's or story character's *intention*. The intention of an act is the goal or purpose. To answer a question about intention, ask yourself, "What goal does this act accomplish?" For example, the intention of a person who adopts a pet is often companionship.

Other TABE questions will ask you to identify the *effect* of an action. *Effect* is another word for result or outcome. When you answer a question about effect, ask yourself, "What was the result or outcome of the act?" Using the earlier pet example, one effect of having a pet is the expense of veterinarian care, food, and other pet supplies.

Example Read this paragraph. What is the mother bear's intention?

_____

What is the effect of her actions? _____

> A mother bear and her cub are feeding on fish on a stream bank. Campers emerge from the forest and surprise the bears. The mother bear stops eating, moves in front of the cub, and roars loudly. The stunned campers back slowly into the forest, where they turn and quickly run to their campsite.

Did you write that the mother bear acted to protect her cub? The bear's intention could be inferred by her change of position and loud roar. You probably also wrote that the bear's actions caused the campers to run away—the effect.

Test Example

Read the paragraph. Answer each question by circling the letter of the best answer.

> In early March, the male robin returns to the park and busily chases other male robins from the area. Within a week, the female joins the male and, together, they collect mud and grass for a nest.

1 In the first sentence, what is the *intention* of the male robin?

   A to make friends

   B to remove competition

   C to locate worms

   D to welcome children

2 Which is an *effect* of the robin pair's actions?

   F They are set to fly south for the winter.

   G They can now store food.

   H They can now find mates.

   J They are ready to lay and hatch eggs.

1 B Because the sentence mentions specifically *male* birds, it makes sense that the robin intends to eliminate any who might compete for his mate before she arrives. Option A is incorrect, since forcing others to leave by chasing them away doesn't suggest friendliness. Options C and D are not logical choices since the sentence does not mention worms or children.

2 J The description of nest building indicates that the birds are preparing to lay and hatch eggs since that is the purpose of a bird's nest. Option A is incorrect since nest building indicates that the birds will remain in the area. Option B is invalid because birds do not use nests to store food. Option C is not logical as the birds have already paired.

Practice

Read the letter that a new dog owner sent to his local animal shelter. Answer the questions by circling the letter of the best answer.

Dear Director Schell,

My family and I adopted Bingo from your shelter six weeks ago. We have grown to love him, but I must admit that we are confused and, sometimes, upset by his behavior. I hope that you will help our family of first-time dog owners better understand Bingo, so that everyone is able to enjoy his presence in our home.

Bingo's barking disturbs the neighbors, which then makes them upset with us. Although he rarely barks when we're home, the neighbors say he barks at people, such as the mailman, who approach our house when my wife and I are at work and the children are in school. What can we do to keep him from barking when people approach our home?

Another problem surfaced only last weekend when we had dinner guests. Throughout the meal, Bingo went from one person to the next, whining and pawing at people's legs. We told him to stop, but he didn't. At the end of the meal, I realized that his nails had actually ripped a hole in my boss's pant leg. How embarrassing! How can we prevent this from happening again?

We realize that most of Bingo's problems result from our lack of experience with dogs. Hopefully, your advice will show us how to teach Bingo proper manners. I know we'll soon be one big, happy family.

Sincerely,
Jason Fortune

1 When Bingo barks at people who approach the house, he intends to

A welcome them

B protect his territory

C play with them

D call the neighbors

2 What is the effect of Bingo's barking?

F Bingo is severely punished.

G No one visits the Fortune home.

H The neighbors are angry.

J Bingo returns to the shelter.

3 An effect of Bingo's behavior near the table is

A job termination

B broken dinnerware

C acid indigestion

D damaged clothing

4 Most likely, Bingo's intention at the table is to

F get food

G play with guests

H punish his owners

J eliminate danger

Check your answers on pages 94–95.

Check your answers on pages 94–95.

Lesson 21 • **57**

Lesson 22 Author's Purpose

Authors write for different reasons or purposes. If you are aware of the intended purpose of what you are reading, you can judge how useful the information is to you.

Example **Read this letter. Why did the author write it?** _____

> To the manager of Berkshire Appliances:
>
> I am looking for a job. I am very handy with tools and I can fix almost anything. I even know how to repair refrigerators and air conditioners. Can you please tell me if your company is hiring right now?
>
> Sincerely,
>
> Greg Davis
>
> Greg Davis

The author wrote the letter to find out if Berkshire Appliances has any job openings. If you were the manager of an appliance store and you needed a repairperson, this letter might be very useful to you.

Test Example

Read this help-wanted advertisement. Answer the question by circling the letter of the best answer.

1 The purpose of writing this advertisement was probably to

A ask a store manager if they need an appliance repairperson

B find a qualified person to work as an appliance repairperson

C let homeowners know whom to call if they need their appliances fixed

D persuade potential employers to contact an appliance repairperson who is looking for a job

> **APPLIANCE REPAIRPERSON NEEDED**
> Repairperson needed to install and repair gas meters, ranges, heaters, air conditioners, and refrigerators in homes and businesses. Applicants must be able to use rulers, pipe cutters, wrenches, and other tools. Responsibilities include collecting money for monthly bills or overdue payments. Apply in person at Berkshire Appliances.

1 **B** The advertisement is intended to let people know that there is a job opening for an appliance repairperson. It lists the skills required for the job as well as a description of the job responsibilities.

Read this article. Answer the questions by circling the letter of the best answer.

Here are three steps you can use to track down jobs and find the one that is just right for you.

Step 1: Look for a Position First you have to know what it is that you are good at and enjoy doing. Look for positions that match your interests, skills, and abilities. Check every resource. Look in the classified section of local newspapers. Look for job postings on the Internet. Ask friends and family members if they know of any job openings in your field.

Step 2: Prepare Your Resume A resume showcases your skills and work experience. Buying a book on how to write a resume is a good investment. Make sure to list skills and qualifications that match the position you are applying for. Remember that you are selling yourself, so it is important to look qualified on paper!

Step 3: Get Ready for Your Interview Before an interview, find out as much as you can about the organization or company. Find out what skills they look for in applicants. Read up on information about them and talk to current employees. Ask intelligent questions during the interview. The idea is to be prepared. After the interview is over, be sure to follow up with a phone call or letter to say thank you. This will impress your potential boss and show that you are truly interested in the position.

1 The author's purpose in writing this article is probably to

A tell a story about finding a job

B teach people how to write a good resume

C challenge employers to create more jobs

D describe how to search for a job

2 The writer probably wants readers to

F agree with a point of view

G find a job that will be a good match

H get more involved in volunteer positions

J tell people how to locate the classified section of the newspaper

3 Which of these is the best title for the passage?

A "Three Tips for Successful Job Hunting"

B "A Resume Showcases Your Skills and Work Experience"

C "Get the Benefits That Are Right for You"

D "How to Conduct Yourself in an Interview"

4 Which of these statements is best supported by the passage?

F If you know your strengths, you can look for a job that matches your skills.

G The more you prepare, the more effective your job search will be.

H A well-written resume will get the attention of potential employers.

J Tracking down opportunities is as easy as 1, 2, 3.

Check your answers on page 95.

Lesson 23 Style Techniques

Authors and writers use different style techniques to convey messages. The techniques used depend on the type of information the author is trying to express. Being familiar with different style techniques will help you to appreciate what you read and help you in your own writing.

Example **Read the paragraph. How does the author try to convince readers to donate blood?** _____

> We all know giving blood helps others, but did you know donating blood is also a healthy habit for yourself? Before donating blood, everyone must pass a physical exam. I was surprised to learn that I had dangerously high blood pressure. Donating blood helped me to be aware of a problem before it had a chance to take my life!

The author described an example and used a personal testimony to convince readers to donate blood. The box below outlines some common style techniques authors use.

Style Technique	What It Is	Example
Concrete Example	a real instance or time that something happened	finding out you have high blood pressure during a physical exam
Exaggerated Details	an overstatement; describing something as greater than it is	The news was so shocking that he tumbled off his chair and almost had a heart attack!
Personal Testimony	when someone testifies or swears to something	"Donating blood made me aware of a problem before it had a chance to take my life!"
Expert Testimonial	when an expert testifies or swears to something	The nurse said, "Getting regular physical exams can mean the difference between life and death."

Test Example

Read the paragraph. Answer the question by circling the letter of the best answer.

> Not paying attention to maintaining your health can cause you major pain and suffering. If you don't go to your doctor for regular physical exams, you could end up getting extremely sick. You might have undiagnosed health problems that will make you deathly ill! If you don't go to the doctor, you have only yourself to blame if you get sick!

Hint

As you read, think about how the author makes a point more convincing or compelling.

1   Which of these techniques does the writer use to describe what could happen to someone who doesn't seek regular medical care?

A   personal testimony

B   exaggerated details

C   concrete example

D   testimonial from an expert

1 B The author uses overstated details to describe what could happen to someone who doesn't seek regular medical care. The description wasn't a real example (option C) or an experience that happened to the author (option A). An expert was not quoted or referred to in this paragraph (option D).

Practice

Read the passage. Answer the questions by circling the letter of the best answer.

During pregnancy, a baby's umbilical cord is the lifeline between it and its mother. After a baby is born, umbilical-cord blood can be a lifeline to others, too. It can be used for medical treatments that can help save the life of a child or adult who has leukemia (bone marrow cancer). I know, because I am a leukemia survivor who benefited from this life-saving technique.

The blood in the umbilical cord helps a baby to grow. It has special cells called "stem cells." Stem cells are also found in bone marrow. Umbilical cords, usually discarded at birth, can help give someone a second chance at life. They are useful in the treatment of leukemia and nearly forty other life-threatening diseases.

Unlike bone marrow, umbilical-cord blood is easy to collect. It can be taken right after birth without risk to the child or mother. It is a simple and painless procedure.

By donating umbilical-cord blood, mothers and their newborn babies can become heroes. And, because there are more than 10,000 babies born in the United States every day, there are at least 10,000 possibilities of hope for leukemia patients around the world.

1 What was the "lifeline" that the author referred to?

A a rope used to save accident victims

B a tube used to give blood to hospital patients

C a life-saving treatment

D a device used to remove the umbilical cord from a newborn baby

2 Which of these techniques does the writer use to convince readers?

F personal testimony

G exaggerated details

H concrete example

J testimonial from an expert

3 What were the "10,000 possibilities of hope" the author referred to?

A the number of stem cells in one umbilical cord

B different kinds of bone marrow

C the babies who are born every day

D all of the possible cancer treatments

4 What was the "second chance at life" the author referred to?

F the possibility of a cure for a deadly disease

G a medicine

H a way of harvesting bone marrow

J a way of giving birth to a baby

Check your answers on page 95.

Lesson 24 Genre

Everything that you read can be classified into a genre, or type of writing. Each genre of writing has its own unique purpose and audience. Being familiar with the different types of writing will help you know where to look for certain information in a library or bookstore. It is also helpful to know about all of the possible reading choices that exist when you read for pleasure.

Example **Read the paragraph. In what type of book would you find a paragraph like this?** _____

> The American Civil War was fought between April 1861 and April 1865. It is one of the most studied conflicts in modern history. The roots of the war go back to the birth of the nation.

A paragraph like this could be found in a history textbook. The different genres of writing generally fall into one of two categories: *fiction* or *non-fiction*. The charts below describe these two categories.

Fiction	Not true; usually tells a story
Formats	Books, novels, and magazine articles

Genres	Themes/Characteristics
Mystery	detectives, secrets, crime
Romance	love, relationships
Science fiction	outer space, the future
Western	cowboys, horses
Fantasy	fantastical fairy tales

Non-Fiction	True; usually gives factual information
Formats	Books, textbooks, magazine articles, news articles and editorials, journals, essays, and reports

Genres	Themes/Characteristics
Informational	topic related
Biographies	about a person's life
Personal narrative	about the author's life

Test Example

Read the paragraph. Answer the question by circling the letter of the best answer.

> The starting pitcher is expected to begin the season on the disabled list. He is recovering from a shoulder injury. The coaches hope to have him back in play by next weekend's game.

TABE **Strategy**

Label what you read as *fiction* or *non-fiction*.

1 This paragraph would most likely be found in

   A a mystery novel

   B a math textbook

   C a daily newspaper

   D an essay about the history of baseball

1 **C** The paragraph is a sports article about a baseball player. The paragraph is non-fiction, so it would not be a novel (option A). The topic is not related to math (option B). An essay about baseball history would not be specific about one player's minor injury (option D).

For numbers 1 and 2, read the passage. Then answer the questions by circling the letter of the best answer.

What do food, clothing, wood, and water all have in common? They all come directly or indirectly from soil. Most of the food we eat comes from the soil. The fibers we use to make some of our clothing come from plants that are grown in soil. Wood comes from trees that hold their roots in soil. Much of the groundwater that we drink is pumped up from the soil.

Soil is a very complex substance that forms very slowly over time. An inch of soil can take hundreds of years to form. If you were to investigate soil under a microscope, you would marvel at the amount of life it contains. A whole ecosystem exists in soil.

1 This passage would most likely appear in

A a cooking magazine

B a science fiction book

C a newspaper editorial

D an introductory text on earth science

2 To find out how to create the best soil for growing vegetables, you would look in

F a daily newspaper

G an article in a gardening magazine

H an advanced textbook on insects that live in the soil

J a novel about a farming community

For numbers 3 and 4, read the passage. Then answer the questions by circling the letter of the best answer.

A disturbance in soil, such as cultivation or adding chemicals, changes the balance of the ecosystem. A change in the soil structure can harm the organisms and animals that live in it. Any change in the soil is reflected in the plants and animals, which are the first to suffer when humans change its composition.

People need to look after and care for soil. Although it is continually being formed, the rate of formation is very slow. This makes it a non-renewable resource. Soil is not just dirt; it is an essential part of the environment. Without healthy soil, we cannot survive.

3 The author's purpose in writing this passage is probably to

A give information about a subject

B report news

C entertain

D tell a story

4 Which of these sentences from the passage expresses an opinion?

F A change in the soil structure can harm the organisms and animals that live in it.

G People need to look after and care for soil.

H A disturbance in soil changes the balance of the ecosystem.

J Soil is a non-renewable resource.

Check your answers on page 95.

Read the passage. Answer the questions by circling the letter of the best answer.

Maya Angelou is best known for her book *I Know Why the Caged Bird Sings,* which was published in 1970. This book tells the story of Maya's own experiences as an African American girl growing up during the Great Depression. It is a story which illustrates that obstacles in life can be overcome with strength and determination.

The story begins with Maya Angelou's birth on April 4, 1928, in St. Louis, Missouri. Her birth name was Marguerite Johnson. She later changed her name to Maya, the nickname her brother gave her as a child. Angelou was her first husband's family name.

When she was three years old, Maya's parents divorced, and she was sent with her brother to live with their grandmother in Arkansas. Maya learned many important life lessons from her grandmother, whom she lovingly called "Momma." Although Maya often dreamed of waking up to see her nappy black hair transformed into long, blonde hair, Momma taught Maya to have pride in herself.

After five years, Maya and her brother were sent back to live with their mother. Things took a turn for the worse when, at age eight, Maya was abused by her mother's boyfriend. The trauma she felt caused her to stop speaking for almost five years. Then Maya moved back to Arkansas, where a woman named Mrs. Flowers helped her rebuild her confidence.

The story ends with the birth of Maya's son, whom she had at the age of 16. Maya's son, Guy, became the new meaning in her life.

I thoroughly recommend the coming of age story *I Know Why the Caged Bird Sings.* It artfully depicts the experience of growing up as an African American in the American South in the 1930s and 1940s. Maya Angelou's talent for putting her soul down onto paper proves that no matter how hard life can get, you can make something of yourself.

1 This passage would most likely be found in

  A a fantasy novel

  B a magazine article

  C an introductory text on creative writing

  D an essay about growing up during the Depression

2 The author's purpose in writing this passage was probably to

  F recommend a good book

  G challenge people to write stories

  H explain how to overcome obstacles

  J persuade readers to agree with a point of view

3 With which of these statements would the author most likely agree?

  A Maya Angelou let the hardships in her life take over.

  B Moving around during one's childhood can be traumatic.

  C Maya Angelou is a gifted writer and an inspirational woman.

  D *I Know Why the Caged Bird Sings* is a dull and boring story.

4 Which outcome can logically be predicted from Maya Angelou's interactions with Mrs. Flowers?

  F Mrs. Flowers adopted Maya Angelou.

  G Maya Angelou borrowed money from Mrs. Flowers.

  H Maya Angelou felt deep gratitude for Mrs. Flowers.

  J Mrs. Flowers raised Maya Angelou's son.

5 Based on the passage, which of these is probably true?

  A Maya Angelou's brother didn't like her.

  B Maya Angelou's grandmother had a negative influence on her.

  C Maya Angelou wanted to get away from her mother's boyfriend.

  D Maya Angelou was depressed when her son was born.

6 Which of these techniques does the author use to illustrate the hardships of Maya Angelou's childhood?

  F concrete examples

  G exaggerated details

  H personal testimony

  J testimonial from an expert

7 Which of these is an opinion?

  A Her first book was about her own experiences.

  B Maya's son, Guy, became the new meaning in her life.

  C Maya learned many important life lessons from her grandmother, whom she lovingly called "Momma."

  D It artfully depicts the real experience of growing up as an African American in the American South in the 1930s and 1940s.

Check your answers on pages 95–96.

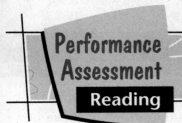
The Reading Performance Assessment is identical to the actual TABE in format and length. It will give you an idea of what the real test is like. Allow yourself 50 minutes to complete this assessment. Check your answers on pages 96–100.

Sample A

When the bright _____ shone directly in our eyes, we couldn't see.

A   sun

B   color

C   shade

D   glasses

Sample B

The sound of breaking glass woke Dave up. The dog started barking. Dave got out of bed, grabbed a baseball bat, and quietly headed downstairs.

Why did Dave get out of bed?

F   The dog needed to be fed.

G   He felt like playing baseball.

H   He needed to fix a broken window.

J   He wanted to find out if someone had broken into the house.

Read the encyclopedia article and study the time line about Social Security. Then answer number 1.

Social Security (*see also Government, United States; Depression, Great; Medicare; Medicaid; Disability Insurance*) The job and money problems of the Great Depression led Congress to pass the Social Security Act in 1935. This law gave payments to workers who lost their jobs. Other parts of the Act helped the elderly, the needy, the disabled, and certain minor children. A 2 percent tax paid for these programs. Half of this tax came out of employees' paychecks; the other half came from their employers. Only the first $3,000 of an employee's earnings was taxed.

Since then, Congress has expanded benefits and added programs, such as Disability Insurance, Medicare, and Medicaid. By 1990, combined payroll tax rates had climbed to 15.3 percent. From its beginning in 1935 to 1990, the maximum Social Security tax burden had grown from $60 to $7,849.

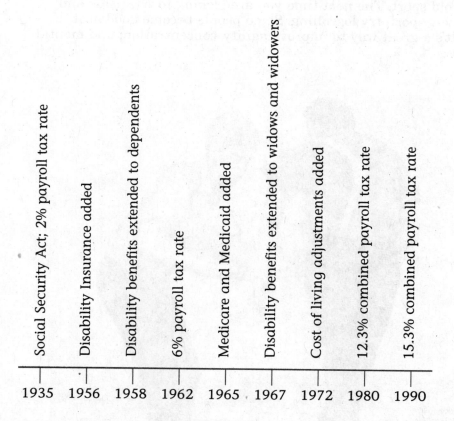

1   Why might a reader refer to the time line in the encyclopedia article?

A   to look for errors in the article

B   to find other sources of information about Social Security

C   to get a quick, visual summary of when events happened

D   to learn who wrote the article

Read the passage. Answer numbers 2 through 6 by circling the letter of the best answer.

The men in early American logging camps knew how to take a break from working. They had a contest that kept everyone in great shape. Two men would stand on a long, round log floating in a river. They would roll the log back and forth until one lost his footing and fell off.

Today, people of all backgrounds enjoy this contest. It has become a popular and competitive sport called logrolling. Logrolling may look simple, but winning a logrolling contest requires focus and balance. It only takes one quick step for an experienced roller to send a beginner plunging into the water.

The key is to not look at your feet because this will throw off your rhythm. If you stick your arms out a bit, you can stabilize yourself. Bending your knees and taking quick steps keeps you in motion. You have to remain on your own end of the log at all times, in between the foul lines, which are painted on the log. Touching your opponent is illegal and will cause you to be disqualified.

Knowing how to swim is the only background needed to learn this 100-year-old sport. The next time you are looking to try a safe and exciting new sport, try logrolling. Some people become good at it quickly! It's a great way to improve agility, concentration, and mental toughness.

2 The author's purpose in writing this passage was probably to

F tell people about a fun and challenging sport

G entertain people with a logging story

H explain how logging camps were run

J persuade people to learn about the history of logrolling

3 Which of these statements is best supported by the passage?

A Loggers are the best logrollers.

B Logrolling is a mental and physical workout.

C People are not interested in logrolling.

D Becoming a logroller requires many years of training.

4 The passage says that bending your knees will "keep you in *motion*." What does the word *motion* mean here?

F power

G energy

H stillness

J movement

5 According to the passage, which of the following techniques is <u>not</u> helpful in logrolling?

A bending your knees

B taking many quick steps

C sticking your arms out to your sides

D focusing your eyes on your feet

6 The way to win a logrolling competition is to

F roll the most logs into a river

G be the first one to stand on a floating log

H be the last one standing on a floating log

J roll a log to the shore in the quickest time

Study this index page from a book about gardening. Then answer numbers 7 through 11 by circling the letter of the best answer.

7 Which of these is listed on page 30?

A Trellises

B Unicorn Plant

C Laying Turf Grass

D Controlling Erosion

8 Which of these is another listing for "Supports"?

F Staking

G Troughs

H Planting

J Tool Sheds

9 Suppose you find several large green worms on your tomato plants and they seem to be eating the tomatoes. On which page will you find information on how to protect your tomatoes from these insects?

A 91

B 145

C 149

D 244

10 If you want to find out what tools you will need to plant your first vegetable garden, on which page will you look for this information?

F 135

G 158

H 210

J 211

11 Which of these <u>cannot</u> be found on this index page?

A Urns

B Stems

C Sundials

D Transplanting

Read the passage about a troublesome insect. Answer numbers 12 through 19 by circling the letter of the best answer.

We have all heard stories of human invasions, both historical and fictional. But, can you believe that an ant is considered to be one of the most damaging invaders that the United States has ever seen? Red imported fire ants are thought to have arrived on the Mississippi or Alabama Gulf Coast in the 1930s, as stowaways on ships from South America. The ants "took over" their new home because there were no natural predators for them to deal with. They thrived on plants, animals, and other insects and multiplied at a rapid rate.

Since their arrival, the ants have infested many of the country's southern states, including Florida, Alabama, and Texas. Many people who live in these places have to contend with the ants' invasions. Fire ants are aggressive and can cause serious harm to people, animals, and crops.

Fire ants are small, red insects that build mounds of soft soil. When their nests are disturbed, they get very agitated. They can quickly swarm up a person's leg and start biting. Each ant can bite repeatedly, so it's possible for someone to endure multiple bites from only a few ants. When the person moves in response to a bite, the movement can trigger even more ants to climb up and attack. The venom that they inject causes a burning and itching sensation. Some bites leave white blisters on the skin that can become infected if not kept clean.

The ants are not only a nuisance to people. They also pose a threat to animals. They are omnivores that feed on small animals as well as plants. They are responsible for killing certain wildlife species, such as quail, deer, lizards, songbirds, and toads. Fire ants have also been known to cause damage to young fruit trees and crops such as corn, okra, and potatoes.

Despite their bad reputation, fire ants are a blessing in disguise to some people. Because the red ant's diet includes insects, they can quickly rid an area of undesired pests. This is good news for areas riddled by ticks. The ants are also helpful in combating termite populations. In addition, they may actually be helpful to some trees by preying on the insects that feed on the tree parts.

However, red imported fire ants continue to have more enemies than friends. There is great hope that in the future we will be able to control the ravages they inflict. In the meantime, fire ants are being controlled by small-scale efforts. Spraying natural and chemical pesticides around and directly onto ant mounds is very effective.

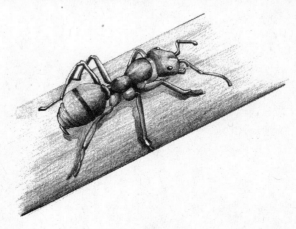

TABE Fundamentals: Reading

12 The author of this passage would probably

F agree that fire ants are a nuisance

G like to see fire ants multiply in numbers

H support research on the benefits of fire ants

J help to introduce fire ants to the northern states

13 The fire ant probably acquired its name because

A it is colored crimson red

B it can only be killed by fire

C its venom produces a burning sensation

D it thrives in hot, desert-like environments

14 Based on the passage, which of the following is probably true?

F Fire ants are a threat to large, domestic animals.

G Some insects are not native to the United States.

H Large populations of fire ants are easy to control.

J Some insects can be trained to be useful to people.

15 Fire ants might be useful to an area that has

A bird nests and a pond

B cornfields and farmlands

C a playground for children

D livestock infested with ticks

16 According to the passage, why do people dislike fire ants?

F They eat termites.

G They have a painful sting.

H They are difficult to destroy.

J They prey on tree-eating insects.

17 Which of these would probably best prevent a skin infection caused by a fire ant?

A rubbing the area vigorously

B putting ice cubes around the area

C washing the area with soap and water

D making a compress using sand and bandages

Numbers 18 and 19 are related to using reference sources. Read each item and circle the letter of the best answer.

18 The quickest way to find the location of the Alabama Gulf Coast would be to look in

F an atlas

G an almanac

H a travel guide

J a magazine

19 Which of these books would probably be the best source of information about how to make natural pesticides?

A *Exploring Nature*

B *Recipes for Organic Gardening*

C *Protecting Our Rivers and Forests*

D *A Field Guide to Beneficial Insects*

Study this rental agreement and read the passage. Use the information to answer numbers 20 through 25.

Rental Agreement

1. Parties
The parties to this Agreement are _____, hereinafter referred to as "Landlord," and _____, hereinafter referred to as "Tenant."

2. Property
Landlord hereby lets the following property to Tenant for the term of this Agreement:
(a) the real property known as: _____ and (b) the following furniture and appliances on said property: _____

3. Term
This agreement shall cover: ___ (a) the period from _____ to _____, or ___ (b) month-to month.

4. Rent
The monthly rental for said property shall be $_____, due and payable on the ____ day of each month.

5. Utilities
Landlord agrees to furnish the following services and/or utilities:
___ Electricity ___ Gas ___ Garbage Collection ___ Snow Removal ___ Water

6. Deposits
Tenant will pay a security deposit in the amount of the first and last month's rental of the property, for a total of $_____ no later than the day before occupancy is assumed. This amount will be refunded within thirty days following the termination of the tenancy; unpaid rent, charges for damages beyond normal wear and tear, and costs for reasonable cleaning may be deducted.

In Addition It Is Agreed:
A. Tenants shall not lease, sublease, or assign the premises without the prior written consent of the Landlord (but this consent shall not be withheld unreasonably).
B. Landlord may enter the premises at reasonable times for the purposes of inspection, maintenance, or repair, and to show the premises to buyers or prospective tenants. In all instances, except those of emergency or abandonment, the Landlord shall give Tenant reasonable notice (at least one day) prior to such entry.
C. Tenant agrees to occupy the premises and shall keep the same in good condition (reasonable wear and tear excepted) and shall not make any alterations thereon without the written consent of the Landlord.
D. Tenant agrees not to disturb the peace and quiet of other tenants in the building. Tenant further agrees not to maintain a public nuisance and not to conduct business or commercial activities on the premises.
E. Tenant shall, upon termination of this Agreement, vacate and return dwelling in the same condition that it was received, less reasonable wear and tear and other damages beyond the Tenant's control.
F. In a dispute between the Landlord and Tenant which gives rise to any action in court, the losing party will pay the court costs and reasonable attorney fees of the successful party.
G. Additional Terms:

We, the undersigned, agree to this Rental Agreement:

Landlord: Tenant:

_____   _____
Name   Name

_____   _____
Signature   Signature

_____   _____
Date   Date

New to the city because of a job transfer, Mai has found an apartment that meets her needs. The apartment manager has given her a *lease*, or written rental agreement, to complete and sign before she can move into the building.

Although she is very excited about the spacious, two-bedroom apartment, Mai knows the importance of reading the rental agreement carefully. She understands that the agreement outlines what she must pay and conditions she must meet. Although the rental agreement is a standard, or ordinary, lease, Mai pays close attention to this consumer material.

20 Which section of the rental agreement describes living costs that may be paid by the landlord?

F Section 6

G Section 5

H Section 4

J Section 2

21 In Section 2 of the lease, the word *lets* means

A rents or leases

B shows or displays

C gives or donates

D sells or trades

22 Based on Section 6, the security deposit may be used to

F install utilities

G pay property taxes

H pay renter's insurance

J repair damages

23 Which section describes what Mai must do if she wishes to move to a different apartment before her rental agreement expires?

A Section 3

B Point E

C Section 4

D Point A

24 Which word or words in Point B protect Mai from surprise inspections by the landlord?

F premises

G reasonable notice

H prospective tenants

J abandonment

25 Which part of the rental agreement restricts Mai's behavior in or around her apartment?

A Point D

B Section 1

C Point F

D Section 2

Read the passage. It is from a story about a woman traveling through China and her stop in Shanghai. Answer numbers 26 through 32 by circling the letter of the best answer.

Walking out of the airport in Shanghai, China, we were directed to a fenced-in walkway surrounded by a crush of people holding signs that we couldn't read and shouting things in Mandarin. I imagine it was a bit like being a professional athlete as they walk out of the tunnel onto the field. It was completely overwhelming. I felt such a rush of emotion that I started crying. I hated this place. I felt so lost and alone in this strange land that was alive with noise and stink and excitement. It was a huge relief to see my uncle John standing there, a head and shoulders taller than everyone else and easy to spot.

We spent two nights in Shanghai, the first of which John took me out to see the city at night. In my wildest dreams I had not imagined the sights we would encounter. Men were riding bikes with metal boxes full of hot coals attached to the back and flat boards full of the most unusual looking (and disgusting) foods-chicken feet, fish heads, intestines . . . definitely not for those with weak stomachs. They cooked it all right there on the street. No health inspections happened here. We decided to be adventurous and bought a kabob of some sort. It tasted dirty and sour. Later I would get sick.

Crowds of people began to follow us as we walked through the streets. The two of us definitely stuck out as foreigners-John with his blond hair and 6'4" stature and me with my pale white skin. Everywhere people were selling all sorts of goods, from knock-off watches to illegally-dubbed DVDs. They were aggressive peddlers. At one point, a man grabbed John's wallet, but John grabbed the guy's arm and shook his wallet loose.

John insisted that we walk to a store he frequented on every trip he'd made to Shanghai. To get there we had to walk into a dark building-home to apartments and businesses-and down an unlit hallway that smelled like rot and fish. It was like something out of a news special. The doorways didn't have doors; instead they were covered by tattered blankets nailed to the wall above them. I could see through and into people's homes. I was afraid. I thought I would relax when we reached the store, but one of the women there was very intrigued by my eyelashes. She grabbed me and touched my eyelashes several times. I felt uncomfortable, violated, attacked, but I don't think my idea of "normal" personal boundaries existed there.

We walked by a temple where people of all ages were praying and chanting. The temple was crowded. It was the 15th day of the lunar cycle, a day that had religious significance unknown to us. We watched in silent reverence as the monks lit incense and blessed packages tied with red ribbons. There was a prayer tree in the center covered with handwritten prayers for the gods to read. I found one written in English that said, "Words cannot convey what I am feeling now, so I leave my soul here on this tree where it belongs. Safe at last." For the first time since arriving in Shanghai, I relaxed. I knew what that note meant.

We stayed out until almost 2 o'clock that morning just walking and watching. I fell in love with the city, its ways, and its customs.

TABE Fundamentals: Reading

26 Which of these is the best title for this passage?

   F "Little Fish in the Big City"

   G "Walking with Uncle"

   H "My Childhood Memories"

   J "Shanghai Nights"

27 Which of these probably happened just before the author found John?

   A She flew into China.

   B She found a wallet.

   C She made a sign.

   D She ate lunch.

28 With which of the following statements would the author most likely agree?

   F Salesmen are always aggressive.

   G All cultures should be respected.

   H Food from bicycle vendors is good.

   J Personal space is overrated.

29 What does the author mean when she says that her idea of "normal" personal boundaries don't exist in Shanghai?

   A People there stay far away from each other.

   B The Chinese tend to get closer to each other than she would prefer.

   C Some people never touch.

   D The Chinese prefer to stay an arm's length away from each other.

30 If the author's sister, upon the author's return home, predicted that Chinese food was fantastic, the author would most likely respond by

   F ignoring her

   G disagreeing and telling her about what people cooked on the back of bikes

   H telling her that they never tried any local food

   J agreeing with her and suggesting they learn how to cook the food she saw

31 Which of these sentences from the passage expresses an <u>opinion</u>?

   A No health inspections happened here.

   B They cooked it all right there on the street.

   C Later I would get sick.

   D It tasted dirty and sour.

32 By the end of the passage, how have the author's feelings for Shanghai changed?

   F from relieved to worried

   G from carefree to cautious

   H from curious to indifferent

   J from fearful to comforted

Go On ▶

Read the letters that a girl and her grandfather sent to one another. Answer numbers 33 through 37 by circling the letter of the best answer.

Dear Grandpa,

How are you? I'm doing great. School is good too. We started a new social studies unit this week. It is about immigration. I really like it so far. One of our homework assignments is to interview someone who came to America from another country. I thought of you as soon as my teacher described the project.

Mom has been telling me stories about how you came to Ellis Island on a boat from Italy. Did you know that you were one of twenty-two million passengers who came through the port of New York between 1892 and 1924? That is amazing! I can't wait to find out more about what it was like to leave your homeland and what you thought of America when you first stepped off the boat.

I miss you, Grandpa, and I can't wait to talk to you. I know that your stories are going to be really interesting. I hope that I can share them with the class. I'll talk to you soon.

Love,
Sophia

Dear Sophia,

I am so glad that you are interested in learning more about your heritage. I would be honored to help you with your school project.

I left Italy as a young boy. Your great grandfather, my father, wanted a better life for his family. That is why he brought us to America.

My first memory of America was seeing the Statue of Liberty, the golden door to the land of opportunity. Lady Liberty stood tall and seemed to welcome all of us on the boat with her glowing torch that lit our way. The boat anchored and we got off and entered the building. We made our way up the steep steps and I was melting. It was August and we were wearing our thick coats, which wouldn't fit in our overstuffed bags.

I have much more to tell you, Sophia. When you call, I will continue with the story. I have plenty of memories to share with you. I may be old, but my mind is as sharp as a tack!

P.S. When I come to visit over the holiday, I would be happy to go to your school and talk with your class. Let me know if you like this idea.

Much love,
Grandpa Tony

TABE Fundamentals: Reading

33 What did Grandpa Tony do when he first got off the boat?

   A He entered the building.

   B He took off his thick coat.

   C He went to his new school.

   D He climbed the steep steps.

34 From reading the letters, you could say that Sophia and her grandfather both

   F want to go to Italy

   G like helping others

   H are interested in family history

   J prefer to travel by boat

35 Why does Grandpa Tony offer to go to Sophia's school?

   A in case she needs a ride home

   B to share his memories with her class

   C because he wants to thank her teacher

   D to talk to her teacher about the homework assignment

36 What was "the golden door" to which Grandpa Tony referred?

   F the door of the boat

   G the Statue of Liberty

   H the door to the building

   J the opportunity for a better life

37 What does the word *interview* mean in Sophia's letter?

   A to meet

   B a news article

   C to congratulate

   D to ask questions

Here is a passage describing an interesting theory about weight loss. Read it and then answer numbers 38 through 43 by circling the letter of the best answer.

Let's imagine a common weight loss scenario. You need to lose weight quickly for a special occasion. Desperate for fast results, you go on the latest "crash" diet that promises to help you lose ten pounds in ten days. Amazingly, when you step on a scale, the display shows that your weight has gone down. But is it body fat that you lost? Probably not. Crash diets are not an effective approach to long-term weight loss. What they mainly do is reduce muscle tissue and the amount of water in your body.

When most people start a diet, they reduce their intake of food and water and become dehydrated. The body stores what water it has in its outer tissues because too little water is being consumed. This water reserve leads to the puffed-up or bloated feeling that we have all felt at one time or another.

While on a diet that urges you to drink lots of water, your weight goes down as the body releases the extra water that has been stored in outer tissues. The bloat disappears now that you are well hydrated, but you have not necessarily lost any fat.

Another way that many crash diets compel your body to lose water weight is by restricting calories. By drastically cutting back on the calories you consume, you lose some of the water that your body has been carrying around. This is especially true of high-protein, low-carbohydrate diets. When you first stop eating carbohydrates, your body releases water that's stored with its supply of carbohydrates. Therefore, most of the weight lost is from water, not fat. If you return to your old eating habits, the water will be stored again and the weight will come right back on.

Now let's talk about muscle tissue. Lean muscle is the body's most active tissue. Muscle burns calories around the clock. The more you have of it, the more calories you will burn. In order to burn fat, lean muscle must be preserved and even strengthened, if possible.

However, most diets do the opposite of this. They force the body into destroying muscle. Crash diets trick the body into thinking that it is starving. Therefore, as a defense, the body attacks itself and begins to burn its lean muscle. By going after muscle tissue, the body is able to stay alive longer while burning fewer food calories each day.

How can you be sure that it is body fat you are losing when the numbers on the scale go down? If you have been drinking plenty of water each day, you can assume that you are well hydrated. This means that the weight loss is not water. Let's also assume that you are maintaining or increasing your muscle mass through strength and resistance training. You can be confident that you are not losing muscle. Therefore, the weight that you are losing must be body fat.

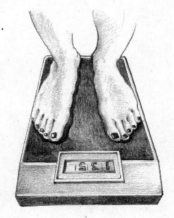

TABE Fundamentals: Reading

38 The *intention* of crash diets is

F lean muscle preservation

G body dehydration

H rapid weight loss

J calorie restriction

39 According to the author of this passage, how might maintaining strength and resistance training affect a person's weight loss program?

A The body would lose weight that is mostly muscle tissue.

B Weight loss would occur because the body would shed extra water weight.

C Muscle mass would remain stable or increase and help the body to burn more calories faster.

D The water supply in the outer tissues of the body would accumulate and cause a person's body to bloat or puff up.

40 Which best describes the *outcome* of a crash diet?

F temporary weight loss

G restored muscle tissue

H increased energy

J increased body strength

41 The fourth paragraph mentions "*restricting calories.*" Which word means the <u>opposite</u> of *restrict*?

A increase

B consume

C acquire

D limit

42 Which of these weight loss plans is most likely to help a person lose body fat?

F Eat more carbohydrates and less protein.

G Drink plenty of water and strengthen muscles.

H Eat plenty of protein and cut back on water intake.

J Consume fewer carbohydrates and stop strength training.

43 Which of these statements best summarizes the excerpt?

A Crash diets are the best way to lose weight.

B Increasing your body's muscle tissue will also increase your body's metabolic rate.

C The key to long-term weight loss is to shed the extra water in your body's outer tissues.

D Long-term weight loss involves increasing your body's muscle tissue and keeping your body well hydrated.

This is a passage about a famous twentieth-century American musician. Read the passage. Then answer numbers 44 through 50 by circling the letter of the best answer.

Ray Charles is one of the most successful musicians of all time. He has several gold records and awards, including a cherished Lifetime Grammy Award. His induction into three different musical Halls of Fame attests to the diversity of his talent.

Ray Charles Robinson didn't start out with many advantages. He was born to Aretha and Baily Robinson on September 23, 1930, during the height of the Depression. In his lifetime Ray Charles not only faced poverty and racial prejudice, but he also had to come to terms with the devastating losses of his family and his vision. Amazingly Ray managed to find the strength to believe in himself and his music, despite the enormous obstacles that were thrown his way.

The first major tragedy in Ray's life was the death of his younger brother. When Ray was five years old, his three-year-old brother drowned in a metal washtub full of water. Ray's childhood trauma intensified when he lost his sight. At age six, he was diagnosed with the degenerative eye disease glaucoma. By age seven, Ray was blind.

The one thing that kept Ray going was his musical studies at St Augustine's School for the Deaf and Blind in Florida. He was admitted to the school on a scholarship. At St. Augustine's, Ray developed his musical gift. He studied classical music, but he felt a passion for jazz and blues. Ray has said that studying classical music was a means to an end. To learn how to arrange and write music, he had to study classical music, but playing jazz and blues was in his heart.

Ray's mother and father passed away, and Ray became an orphan at age 15. He turned to music for comfort and set out on the road to becoming a professional musician. Ray's musical career began to take off after he moved to the west coast. He cut his first professional recording in 1950. The song, "I Got a Woman," became a smash hit.

Ray Charles Robinson shortened his name to Ray Charles, and he traveled around the United States, playing at different clubs. The only damper to his rising success was the racial inequality and segregation with which he had to contend. When he traveled, he had to find gas stations that had restrooms for "colored" people. If he was hungry, he had to find restaurants that would serve blacks.

Once, a show promoter told Ray that he would have to play downstairs to the white audience and the black audience would have to listen from upstairs. Ray cancelled the show and sought moral support in his new friendship with activist Dr. Martin Luther King, Jr. The commitment to King's cause was in Ray's heart. He helped to raise money through his music to fund the legal expenses of people who were jailed for breaking unfair laws.

Ray Charles went on to have one of the most successful careers in American musical history, recording hit after hit. He achieved worldwide fame and had a profound influence on popular music.

44 This passage would most likely be found in

F a blues magazine

G an introductory text on classical music

H a political newspaper column

J an essay about racial injustice

45 Which of these is probably true of Ray Charles?

A He is best known for his country and western music.

B He could compose music only when he was happy.

C He was influenced by the musical styles of classical performers.

D He became more determined to fight racial injustice as he experienced it in his own life.

46 What did he mean when he said that studying classical music was a means to an end?

F It would give him the training he needed to learn to write and arrange music.

G It allowed him to develop himself as a classical musician.

H He wanted it to end.

J He really wanted to study the blues.

47 According to the passage, Ray Charles acted on a *commitment* to King's cause. In this context, the word *commitment* means the same as

A pledge

B calling

C witness

D yearning

48 Which of these best describes Ray Charles's reaction to the way that he was treated while on tour?

F He was amused by the requests of certain show promoters.

G He was angry because many restaurants didn't have the foods he liked.

H He was overjoyed to have the freedom to travel and stay wherever he wanted.

J He was upset that there were separate facilities for people of different races.

49 According to the passage, what did not happen in Ray Charles's life?

A His father died.

B His mother died.

C His brother died.

D He was hauled into jail.

50 Which of these best summarizes the passage?

F Ray Charles composed and recorded many classical hits during his lifetime.

G Ray Charles showed his respect for Dr. Martin Luther King, Jr., by joining in his protest rallies.

H Ray Charles, a musician, overcame tragic events and shared his gift of music with the world.

J Ray Charles lost his family members and devoted his life to writing about them in his books and recordings.

Read this passage about sleep disorders. Answer numbers 51 through 55 by circling the letter of the best answer.

Nearly one in every four Americans has trouble sleeping. Of these, half have ongoing sleep problems. Sleep disorders can begin suddenly or develop over time. Some problems are due to physical or emotional illness or disease; others are the result of a situation. For example, people with busy schedules may have difficulty relaxing enough to fall asleep. Others may have jobs that require them to work at night when they are used to sleeping. Some may continually change work shifts, working nights one week and days the next. Still others fight a biological battle. Their internal clocks may not coincide with assigned work schedules; a "night owl," for example, may not be able to fall asleep at 8 p.m. and rise at 4 a.m. for work.

Most people with ongoing sleep problems have one of four disorders: insomnia, sleep apnea, narcolepsy, or restless legs syndrome. People who have trouble falling or staying asleep, but are sleepy during the day, have insomnia. In most cases, insomnia is caused by an emotional problem or other health condition.

People with sleep apnea are also sleepy during the day, but they frequently snore loudly at night. Sleep is interrupted when the person stops breathing for short periods and awakens gasping for breath.

Narcolepsy is a disorder in which people cannot regulate their sleeping and waking hours. They may fall asleep at any time and any place and are often sleepy in the daytime. Their nighttime sleep is interrupted. Their muscles may sometimes become weak or paralyzed.

Restless legs syndrome, or RLS, also interrupts sleep. Because their legs tingle when they sit or lie down, people with RLS must constantly move or stretch their legs to relieve symptoms.

Sleep disorders are no laughing matter. Without enough sleep, people are more likely to have accidents, perform poorly in school or at work, and experience frequent bad moods. Many treatments are currently available, and more will come as research continues.

51 After reading this passage, someone with sleep problems would probably

    A change jobs

    B sleep more

    C see a doctor

    D buy a new bed

52 Read the sentence and the question to decide on an appropriate word for the blank.

The future of people with sleep disorders looks＿＿＿＿＿＿＿＿＿ as doctors and researchers look for cures and treatments.

Which word completes the idea that there is hope for people with sleep disorders?

    F promising

    G depressing

    H cunning

    J taxing

53 According to the article, which of the following causes people with sleep apnea to awaken?

    A bright daylight

    B leg discomfort

    C gasping for breath

    D emotional problems

54 Which generalization about the passage is most accurate?

    F Sleep disorders have a variety of causes.

    G Sleep disorders affect few people.

    H Doctors are unconcerned about sleep disorders.

    J People can correct their own sleep disorders.

55 The first paragraph of the passage states that many people "have *ongoing* sleep problems." Which word means the <u>opposite</u> of *ongoing*?

    A continuing

    B delightful

    C trivial

    D occasional

STOP

Lesson 1 Practice (page 9)

1. **B** The topic "Siding" and the sub-topic "Patching" are on page 35. Information about repairing a subfloor is not what is needed (option A). Information about completely removing or taking off vinyl siding is not required for repairing only a small hole (option C). Information about vinyl tiles is not needed (option D).

2. **J** The topic "Two-slot Receptacle" is *not* listed on this index page. Options F, G, and H are not correct because each of those topics is listed on this index page.

3. **C** The topic "Suspended Ceilings" is found on page 208. Options A, B, and D are not correct because information on those topics *cannot* be found on page 208. Different page numbers are assigned to those topics.

4. **F** The page number for bathroom sinks is located under the topic "Sinks" and under the sub-topic "Bathroom" on page 228. Option G is not correct because information on *kitchen* sinks is on page 225. A kitchen sink may require a different type of drain than a bathroom sink. Options H and J are not correct because neither option has to do with sinks.

Lesson 2 Practice (page 11)

1. **C** A book of quotations would probably have the *most* sayings by a famous president. Options B and D are not correct because these sources don't have many sayings. Option A is not correct because an atlas does not contain sayings.

2. **F** The *fastest* way would be to look in an atlas for a map of the state of Virginia. Options G and J are not correct because these sources don't usually have state maps in them. Option H is not correct because a magazine probably wouldn't have a state map either.

3. **B** To give credit to a source, use a footnote. In option A, just highlighting a quotation would not show where it came from. In option C, an author's name does not belong *at the top* of a report. In option D, putting all of the author's books in a bibliography would not show where a particular quote came from.

4. **H** The book called *Thomas Jefferson's Inventions* would have the *most* information about the inventions of Jefferson. A book about architecture and building designs (option F), a book about writing (option G), or a book about copy machines (option J) would not be useful.

5. **B** An encyclopedia offers brief, yet comprehensive, articles on a range of subjects and topics. Atlases (option A) and anthologies (option D) do not offer information on people. A book of quotations (option C) would only offer Jefferson's notable quotes.

6. **H** A local real estate weekly magazine would be a very useful resource. Options F, G, and J do not offer local real estate information.

Lesson 3 Practice (page 13)

1. **C** The meal with cheese and milk would furnish the most calcium (50% of the RDA). Peanut butter and milk (option A) provides 30%, while roast beef and juice (option B) and peanut butter and juice (option D) supply no calcium.

2. **G** Since high amounts of sodium are not healthy, Jorge would probably not pack a roast beef sandwich. Roast beef actually has *more* protein per serving than peanut butter or cheese, so option F is incorrect. Similarly, roast beef has *fewer*, not *more*, calories than peanut butter or cheese, so option H is incorrect. Finally, option J is incorrect since a serving of roast beef has less fat than either peanut butter or cheese.

3. **A** The cranberry-blueberry juice furnishes 100% of the Recommended Daily Allowance (RDA) of Vitamin C. Cheddar cheese (option B) provides only 6% Vitamin A and 20% of the mineral calcium. Peanut butter (option C) supplies no vitamins and only 2% of the iron RDA. While milk (option D) supplies Vitamins A (10%), C (4%), and D (25%), as well as 30% of the calcium RDA, milk fails to furnish 100% of the Recommended Daily Allowance of any vitamin or mineral.

4. **J** Four of the foods—milk, juice, cheese, and beef—contain 0 grams of fiber. The fat-free milk is the only food that does not provide fat (option F). Of the five foods, only cranberry-blueberry juice supplies no protein (option G). Only two of the foods fail to provide carbohydrates (option H): cheddar cheese and roast beef.

1. B The Lichterman Nature Center features birds, reptiles, amphibians, and mammals. Options A, C, and D refer to historical and cultural museums. [Consumer Materials]

2. J If the family does not vacation over Labor Day weekend, it cannot view the Memphis Music and Heritage Festival. The festival offers nonmusical attractions, such as dancers, cooks, artists, and talkers so option F is not accurate. The brochure does not mention cost (option G). All attractions are in Memphis; the brochure does not describe location, so option H is not verifiable. [Consumer Materials]

3. A The brochure describes the Children's Museum as a place where *children* can interact with exhibits, while the other attractions are billed for families, adults, and schoolchildren—people of all ages. The title of the brochure page, *Memphis Highlights*, suggests that all of the attractions are located in Memphis (option B). All museums in the brochure have exhibits (option C). Based on the descriptions of each attraction, all could be considered educational (option D). [Consumer Materials]

4. H Page 76 can be found under the heading of *Smith, Junior,* and then under the sub-heading of *recording sessions.* In option F, page 29 has information on Junior Smith and *Elvis's army service.* In option G, page 33 has information on recordings with Gordon Stoker. In option J, page 99 has information on TV appearances with Ed Sullivan. [Index]

5. C The book of quotations is the only reference source listed that contains sayings. An almanac lists facts and statistics (option A), while an encyclopedia contains articles that may or may not include quotations (option B). An anthology is a collection of writings, not a collection of sayings (option D). [Reference Sources]

6. F The word *Life* in the title of *The Life and Times of the King of Rock 'n' Roll* indicates that this is the title of a life story, or biography. The last words of *From the Blues to Rock 'n' Roll: A Musical History* (option G) suggest that this book focuses on music development, not a life story. While Elvis may have been featured in *Famous Southerners of the Twentieth Century* (option H), the title suggests that the book is not devoted to only his life story. A cookbook—*Peanut Butter and Bananas: An Elvis Cookbook* (option J)—is not likely to contain Elvis's life story. [Reference Sources]

1. C The word *whipping* in this paragraph means "blowing." It makes sense because wind blows. *Whipping* also means "beating" (option A), but that answer does not fit with the meaning of the sentence. *Whipping* can mean "mixing," but that answer does not fit with the meaning of the sentence (option B). Option D is not correct because *whipping* does not mean "singing."

2. J The word *adorned* in this paragraph means "decorated." It makes sense because wings are decorated with feathers. *Adorned* does not mean the same as *adhered, admired,* or *traveled* (options F, G, and H).

3. B The word *scanned* in this paragraph means "searched." It makes sense because searching means the same as *looking,* another word in the sentence. In one context, *scanned* can mean *copied* (option A), but that answer does not fit with the meaning of the sentence. *Scanned* does not mean the same as *swindled* or *traversed* (options C and D).

4. G The word *determined* in this paragraph means "steadfast." It makes sense to say: "The urgency of my search kept me focused and determined *(steadfast).*" *Determined* does not mean the same as *awake, defeated,* or *delighted* (options F, H, and J).

5. D The word *effortlessly* in this paragraph means "without force." It makes sense to say: "floating effortlessly *(without force)* through the cold night air." *Effortlessly* does not mean the same as "without pain" (option A), "without warmth" (option B), or "without warning" (option C).

6. H The word *tingle* in this paragraph means "a prickling sensation." It makes sense to say: "the tingle *(a prickling sensation)* of hunger." *Tingle* does not mean the same as "a cold sensation" (option F), "a sudden movement" (option G), or "a feeling of alertness" (option J).

1. C A demotion is a reduction in rank or status, the opposite of a *promotion,* or advancement in rank or status. The words *advancement* (option A) and *upgrade* (option B) are incorrect because both describe going from a lesser to a greater state and mean the same as *promotion* in some contexts. Although the words *promotion* and *commotion* share a base word that means "movement," a promotion means going or putting forward or in a better position, while a commotion is a disorderly, disorganized, or tumultuous movement.

2. F The word *intangible* comes from the Latin words for "not" and "to touch"; consequently, the opposite of "not to touch" is *touchable*. *Abstract* (option G) and *unreal* (option H) are synonyms of *intangible* as both describe concepts or things that are not real or touchable. The word *terrible* (option J) means "horrible" or "awful" and is neither synonymous nor antonymous with *intangible*.

3. A The word *current* in this context means "present" or "contemporary," the opposite of *former*, which means "past" or "earlier." While a former president may be deceased or dead (option B), the word *former* indicates order or sequence, not living status. *Previous* (option C) means the same as *former*. The word *respected* (option D) means "held in high esteem or regard" or "revered." It does not indicate order or sequence, so this choice is incorrect.

4. J A sound or functioning item works well, the opposite of one that is *faulty*. The words *defective* and *impaired* (option F) and *unfit* and *flawed* (option G) are synonyms of *faulty*. While something that is ancient or old (option H) may not work well and, consequently, could be considered faulty, the assumption cannot be automatic, so this response is incorrect.

Lesson 6 Practice (page 21)

1. B The word *sources* is synonymous with the clue word *supplies* in the question. The word *uses* (option A) is not correct because the article describes a potential shortage of water for existing uses; new uses would put an even bigger strain on water resources. The word *kinds* (option C) does not make sense in the context of the sentence. *Flavors* (option D) does not complete the idea that new supplies of water may be necessary.

2. H A *repair* will stop a faucet from leaking. *Notice* (option F) is not correct because simply seeing that a faucet is leaking will not stop the leak. Although the *purchase* (option G) of a new faucet enables one to replace a leaky faucet, it does not stop the original faucet from leaking. The word *install* (option J) does not correctly complete the sentence because the act of installing, or putting into position, a faucet would not stop a leak.

3. A The word *limit* in the question is a synonym of the correct response—*restrict*. The word *produce* (option B) is not correct because governments cannot produce, or make, water. *Increase* (option C) is also incorrect; if governments were to increase water usage, shortages would grow worse, not diminish. *Ignore* (option D) is not an appropriate word in this context. If the government ignores (or refuses to acknowledge) water usage limitations, the water shortage problem will become worse.

4. G The word *conserve* means to "save or hold in reserve through wise usage," which completes the idea of the sentence. *Consume* (option F) is incorrect because, while it indicates usage, it does not suggest the type (wise/unwise) of usage. The words *connect*, or link (option H), and *construct*, or build (option J), do not make sense in the sentence.

TABE Review: Words in Context (pages 22–23)

1. B In this sentence the word *aroma* means "scent." The author could smell the scent of the chicken cooking. Options A and D are words that have to do with eating, and the passage doesn't mention eating the chicken until the second paragraph. Option C is not correct because aroma has to do with the sense of smell, not sight.

2. H In this sentence the word *indulge* means "to gratify" or "satisfy." The author was indulging, or gratifying, herself or himself by eating the drumstick. In option F *indulge* in this context does not mean "to eat," although eating is one form of indulgence. In option G "to cover" means "to hide." In option J "to embrace" means "to hold."

3. D Since the word *emerged* in this sentence means "came out or forth into sight," the word *disappeared* (or vanished from sight) means the opposite. *Originated* (option A) is not an antonym, as it means "began or originated from." The word *escaped* (option B) means "fled or left as if from danger"; while it describes leaving, not coming forth, it has additional connotations that disqualify it as an antonym of *emerged*. The word *proceeded* (option C) means "came forth," so its meaning is similar to that of *emerged*.

4. H The word *drag* means "move slowly" in the context of this sentence. *Slow-motion* is a clue. It means slow movement. Although "pull" (option F) and "search" (option G) are correct definitions for the word *drag*, they do not fit with the meaning of the sentence. Option J is not correct because it contradicts the meaning of *slow motion*.

5. A The word *vivid* means "clear or bright," and completes the idea of a detailed memory. *Vague* (option B) means "insubstantial or unclear," the opposite of a word that suggests a clear recollection. *Dreadful* (option C), which means "awful," is incorrect because it suggests that the writer's memories were unpleasant, while the passage describes fond memories. The word *occasional* (option D) refers to frequency; an occasional memory happens once in a while. This word does not complete the idea of clarity of recollection.

6. F The word *exposed* means "visible," The word *concealed*, which means "hidden or not visible," would be the opposite. The other answers all mean the same as *exposed*.

7. A The word *unsettled* means "uneasy" in the context of this sentence. The author was uneasy, or uncomfortable, with the way his grandmother's stockings looked. The opposite would be *comfortable*. *Uneasy* (option B) and *not paid* (option C) both mean the same as *unsettled*. *Happy* is different than *unsettled,* but it does not mean the opposite.

8. G The word *mimicked* means "imitated" or "copied." The children wanted to imitate, or act like, their grandfather. The children in the story were not trying to entertain or amuse (option F) their grandfather. They were not trying to annoy or irritate (option H) him either. Their grandfather wasn't meeting anyone in the story so he didn't need to be introduced (option J).

1. D The second paragraph states that Spanish explorers brought horses to North America. Option A is not correct because *sky dogs* is what the horses were called. Option B is not correct because although the Native Americans believed that the Great Spirit was responsible for the horses, they were actually brought by the Spanish. In option C, the Native Americans did not bring horses to the Plains. They just owned and used them.

2. F The first paragraph states that "the early Native Americans of the Plains traveled and hunted on foot." Traveling *on foot* means walking. Dogs were used to pull supplies, not for riding (option G). The *early* Native Americans couldn't have used horses (option H) because they didn't have horses before the Spanish brought them. The passage does not mention wagons (option J).

3. C The last paragraph describes how horses "increased the supply of food and improved mobility." Option A is not correct because the passage does not mention how the horses looked. Option B is not correct because horses were believed to be a gift from the Great Spirit, not brought by people. Just because the horses were compared to dogs (option D) was not enough of a reason to cherish them.

4. G The last paragraph states that "horses could also pull heavier loads than the dogs." Options F, H, and J are incorrect because the passage does not mention that horses were used to train dogs, carry children, or guard teepees.

5. D The second paragraph says that the horses were thought to be large dogs, "sent as a gift from the Great Spirit of the sky." The passage does not mention that the horses chased dogs (option A). In option B, horses are compared to dogs, not birds. Although the horses were believed to be a gift, the passage did not state that they were thought to have fallen from the sky (option C).

1. C The first thing that Lance did after his recovery from cancer was to get back into shape. According to the passage, Lance got married *after* he began getting back into shape (option A). The birth of Lance's baby happened *last* in the passage (option B). Lance won the Tour de France as a result of, or *after*, getting back into shape (option D).

2. J The passage says that Lance got married in 1998. This happened *before* July and October of 1999 (options F and G). Option H is not correct because he won the Tour de France in July of 1999, during the year *after* his marriage.

3. A Lance got back into shape *after* his recovery from cancer, not before he got sick with cancer (option B). Option C is not correct because Lance's baby was born after the Tour de France. Option D is not correct because Lance got back in shape *before* winning the Tour de France.

4. G The *last* event that happened in this passage was that Lance's baby was born. All the other events in the passage (options F, H, and J) happened before Luke's birth.

1. D The companies that make and sell BGH would make the most money. Options A and C are not correct because the federal government would use taxpayers' money to offset the costs related to a surplus of milk. Option B is incorrect because small dairy farms would *not* benefit. In fact, some would be forced out of business.

2. H The article says that "BGH has been linked to cancer and other diseases in dairy cows." Options F and G are not correct because the article does not say that BGH makes cows more fertile or aggressive. Option J is incorrect because BGH *increases*, not *decreases*, the milk production of dairy cows.

3. D The last paragraph states that "the government will have to buy the additional milk." It goes on to say that this money would come from the taxpayers. The article doesn't say that the surplus in milk will bring prices down (option A). The article doesn't make any statement regarding health benefits to taxpayers (option B). If small dairy farmers go out of business, there may be *fewer* brands of milk on supermarket shelves (option C).

4. F The first paragraph says that "Canada has banned the use of BGH." Option G is not correct because if Canada has dairy farms, then Canadian dairy farms *could* have a need for a product that would help increase the supply of milk. Options H and J are not correct because they contradict the information in the paragraph.

TABE Review: Recall Information (pages 30–31)

1. C The article suggests changing your routine in order to "shock" the muscles and get past a plateau. Options A and D are not correct because the article doesn't mention running or doing repetitions. Option B contradicts what the article says about increasing the amount of weights you use. [Stated Concepts]

2. J The article gives examples of how to change your routine. One example suggests using the leg press once every ten days if you currently use it once every five days. Options F and H are not correct because adding more weight or using more free weights is not mentioned in reference to the leg press. The article doesn't suggest stopping exercise altogether (option G). [Details]

3. D The second paragraph says that "it's common to plateau by doing the same thing again and again." A plateau is when you stop seeing results. In option A, using the weight-lifting circuit wouldn't be a reason to plateau. In option B, bodybuilders would *start* seeing results if they tried new workouts. In option C, food isn't mentioned in the article. [Stated Concepts]

4. G "Shock training" is described in the article as varying or changing your workout routine. The third paragraph gives the example of replacing bench presses with some flies. Options F and H are not correct because neither food nor friends are mentioned in the article. Option J is not correct because doing the same routine would contradict the main point of the article. [Details]

5. A The first paragraph describes how Arnold was upset or unhappy "because his father never praised his best efforts." Option B contradicts this information. In option C, the passage doesn't mention whether or not Arnold's father came to his competitions. Option D is not correct because Arnold's father did not want Arnold to be a bodybuilder, and he most likely didn't want to be one himself. [Stated Concepts]

6. H The last paragraph says that Arnold was 20 years old when he won first place in the Mr. Universe Competition. Option F is not correct because in 1966 Arnold won *second* place in the Mr. Universe Competition. Option G is not correct because Arnold was 18 when he joined the army. Option J is not correct because Arnold won the competition *after* he joined the army. [Sequence]

7. C The second paragraph says that Arnold broke into the gym to work out. Options A and B are not correct because the passage doesn't say he went home or waited outside. The passage doesn't mention a second gym (option D). [Details]

8. H The first sentence says Arnold was born in Austria. Germany, France, and Belgium (options F, G, and J) are not mentioned in the passage. [Details]

Lesson 10 Practice (page 33)

1. A In the first paragraph, Linda writes to Carlos that they "used to joke around." The paragraph doesn't mention what kind of food Carlos and Linda like to eat (option B). Carlos already has a job working at the shelter (option C). Option D is incorrect because although Linda may have had trouble sleeping in her car, the letter doesn't mention how Carlos sleeps.

2. H In her letter, Linda mentioned that the scariest time in her life was when she had to sleep in her car. That was probably why she went to stay at the shelter. She had to sell her furniture for money and because she no longer had a place to keep it (option F). Linda could joke around with Carlos when she was living at the shelter, and her life wasn't going smoothly then (option G). Option J is incorrect because the letter doesn't mention Linda's health.

3. D Linda seemed grateful and thankful that the Lodge was there when she was going through a tough time. The letter didn't mention that the Lodge was

closing (option A). Linda mentions Carlos joking with her and the kindness shown to her (option B). Linda writes that when she was able to get an apartment, she was glad "to get back on [her] feet again" (option C).

1. B The passage is mostly about the life of Jacques Cousteau, a famous inventor and underwater explorer. Options A and D are incorrect because the TV show and the Cousteau Society were mentioned only to highlight accomplishments in Cousteau's life. Option C is incorrect because the passage doesn't tell about *how* the mines were used. It tells about how the aqua-lung was used to detect mines.

2. J The passage is a short summary or description of Jacques Cousteau's life. The passage doesn't give details about *Calypso* (option F). Cousteau (option G) didn't write the passage. It was written about him. Option H is incorrect because the only famous French explorer mentioned is Cousteau.

3. A Cousteau's life was devoted to the ocean. He educated others on this topic by writing books, making movies, and inventing equipment that show what life is like in the ocean. Options B and D are incorrect because fighting in World War II and having a family are only briefly mentioned in the passage. Option C is incorrect because Cousteau *invented* the aqua-lung. The passage didn't say that he taught people how to use it.

4. H The first sentence of the fourth paragraph answers the question. Option F is not correct because 1910 is the year Cousteau was born. Option G is not correct because 1933 is the year Cousteau joined the French Navy. Option J is not correct because 1997 is the year Cousteau died.

1. B This summary includes the *subject*: the job of an animal control worker; the *action*: using pet microchips; and the *outcome*: locating pet owners faster. The passage doesn't mention anything about how hard it is to find people to do the job (option A). Options C and D are incorrect because

they are facts from the passage; they don't include enough information to be complete summaries.

2. H Option H summarizes how the chips make it easier to reunite lost pets with their owners. Options F, G, and J are details, but are not the main reason why the chips make finding a lost pet's owner easier.

3. D According to the passage, animal control workers have to catch animals, transport them to shelters, and fill out paperwork to help locate pet owners. Option A is incorrect because the workers don't enter information into the database; they access or use it. Options B and C are job descriptions that are not included in the passage.

1. C The passage states that if someone has a large tumor on the larynx, it could result in the removal of the voice box. A history of smoking (option A) or a small neck lump (option B) is not reason enough to remove the voice box. The passage does not say anything about removing a voice box if a person cannot communicate (option D).

2. G The passage refers to a special device that can help a person speak. It does not say that the device is a computer with a mechanical voice (option H). Option F is not true; a person cannot get a new voice box. Laser surgery (option J) is used to treat some kinds of throat cancer, but it is not used to help with speech.

3. A The fourth paragraph includes information to support the statement in option A. Options B, C, and D are not supported by the passage.

4. F It is a good idea to quit smoking because the damage tobacco smoke causes can turn into cancer. Options G, H, and J are all true statements, but they are not the most important reason to quit. Avoiding cancer is the most important reason to quit.

1. D In the beginning, Jennifer felt homesick for holiday traditions. After Diego told her that they celebrate similar traditions in her new neighborhood, she felt comforted. Options A, B, and C are not supported by the passage.

2. **G** Jennifer and Diego both talked about memories of the same holiday traditions. Options F, H, and J are not supported by the passage.

3. **B** The passage is about a woman realizing that you can feel at home wherever you are. Option A is not the main idea of the passage, and it is not true. Options C and D are both true details from the passage, but they do not summarize the entire passage.

4. **J** Jennifer was homesick because she missed holiday traditions that were special to her. Options F and G are not reasons why she would be homesick. There is nothing in the passage to support the statement in option H.

Lesson 15 Practice (page 43)

1. **B** The salamander crossing is made up of two tunnels that allow salamanders to safely cross the road in order to get to the pond. The crossing is for salamanders to use, not for people to use (options A and D). The crossing is not a warning sign (option C) for the tunnel.

2. **H** The passage said that the "critters were getting squashed by careless drivers." This means they were getting run over by cars. The passage didn't say that the salamanders found another route (option F) or that they laid their eggs in puddles (option G). It didn't mention police officers (option J).

3. **A** The sign shows the location of the tunnels that the salamanders use to migrate to the pond. The entrance to the tunnels is below the sign. The sign is not to warn drivers to slow down (options B and D). The salamanders are no longer in danger now that they have tunnels. The sign marks the location of the tunnels, not the pond (option C).

4. **H** The article says that the residents were "relieved" that the salamander crossing was built. Putting slots in the tunnels (option F), parking at the train station (option G), and the distance between the tunnels (option J) are not ways that residents showed "relief."

Lesson 16 Practice (page 45)

1. **B** These facts are both in the passage and they support the statement. Althea rose to the top of the tennis world even though she grew up poor. Option A is incorrect because the passage doesn't say that Althea graduated from high school. The facts in options C and D are in the passage, but they don't support the statement because they are not examples of "rising to the top."

2. **H** According to this passage, the sport did not immediately recognize Althea based on her skill alone. The passage does not have information to support options F and J. Option G contradicts information in the passage; when she started playing, Althea did not have access to good coaches.

3. **D** Option D is the best answer because Althea was banned from most public tennis courts early in the story, and she became the top player in the world at the end of the story. Option A is not correct because Althea was not ignored at the end of her career. Options B and C are not correct because Althea was not celebrated or acknowledged early in her career.

TABE Review: Construct Meaning (pages 46–47)

1. **C** The author describes the story of how his family acquired their family home. "The Story of My Life" (option A) is not correct because the passage is not all about the author's life. Option B is incorrect because it includes just a little information about life as a migrant worker. The passage does not describe how to grow fruits and vegetables (option D). [Main Idea]

2. **G** Habitat for Humanity helped the author's family build a house that they otherwise would not have been able to afford. Habitat for Humanity builds permanent homes for families, not temporary homes for migrant workers (option F). Option H is not the best answer because Habitat for Humanity serves and helps families; the volunteers just provide the work. Option J is incorrect because Habitat for Humanity is about housing, not farming. [Conclusion]

3. **D** The author's father said he wanted a better life for his family. The author's father didn't lose his job (option A); he quit it. He got a job in a grocery store (option B) after he made the decision to settle down. The statement in option C is not supported by the passage. [Cause and Effect]

4. **F** The mother wanted to "raise a family and teach our children the value of education." This means that she wanted her own children to go to school. She wanted her own house, not her own farm (option G). The author's mother did not want to move back into her parents' house (option H).

Option J is incorrect because she paid for her own college tuition. [Conclusion]

5. **C** The last two paragraphs are about how the organization Habitat for Humanity improved the living situation of the author's family. Option A is not the best answer because the passage is the story of one family, not one town. Option B is incorrect because the author's father did not go to college. The man and the woman in the passage do not live in Mexico (option D). [Summary]

6. **G** Before the author's father had a family of his own, he seemed content with living as a migrant worker. When his family started to grow, he became dissatisfied with his job; he wanted a better life. The father was not bored (option F), disenchanted (option J), or resentful (option H) anywhere in the passage. [Compare and Contrast]

7. **D** The first paragraph states that for the author's father, home was wherever the next harvest was. Option A is incorrect because the house was simple, not expensive. If option B were true, then the family wouldn't have needed Habitat for Humanity's help. The passage contradicts option C. The passage does not mention the author's mother's home. [Supporting Evidence]

8. **H** The father's old and new jobs both have to do with produce, but the new job does not require him to move from farm to farm. Option F is incorrect because both jobs involve working with food. Option G is incorrect because working in a grocery store doesn't involve traveling. Option J does not reflect the meaning of the quote. [Conclusion]

9. **A** Option A is correct because he considered his family's welfare first and decided to settle down after he got married. The passage does not say that he prefers traveling (option B). Option C is not supported by the passage. The passage does not mention whether he enjoys building houses. [Character Aspects]

10. **G** The passage supports this statement. Option F is not true; the family does know its history. Option H is not correct because it is not true. Option J is not correct because the house is "simple but sturdy," not fancy. [Character Aspects]

Lesson 17 Practice (page 49)

1. **A** The word *spectacular* indicates an opinion or a personal view of the author. Options B, C, and D are all facts that are stated in the letter.

2. **J** According to the letter, the park was, in fact, donated by Percival P. Baxter. Options F and G are opinions. Option H is neither a fact nor an opinion. It is a request from the author to the readers of the letter.

3. **C** Not everyone may feel that logging would ruin the park's beauty. According to the letter, Baxter State Park is located in Maine (option A). Ponds are sometimes used for fishing and canoeing (option B). According to the letter, people do hike and camp in Baxter (option D).

4. **J** Option J is a fact because all these animals do live in the park. Options F and H include the word *should*, which is used to express an opinion. Option G includes the word *important*, which is an opinion word.

Lesson 18 Practice (page 51)

1. **B** The exhausted collapse of a man who has run 25 miles nonstop is a predictable outcome based on the reader's knowledge and experience. Based on the same knowledge and experience, the idea that a person can add another 25-mile run immediately afterward (option A) is not likely. Since the runner is a Greek soldier who risks exhaustion to announce the victory of his army over the Persians, the prediction that the soldier will defect to the enemy army (option C) does not make sense. A soldier on an important mission is unlikely to forget what he was sent to do when he arrives (option D).

2. **J** The ending keywords *more marathon races* and *contests of athletic skill, strength, and endurance* describe the Olympic Games that developed from the idea of the Ancient Greek games. Both the Cannes Film Festival (option F) and the Academy Awards (option G) honor people involved in filmmaking, not athletic contests. While the Super Bowl (option H) is a sporting contest, it did not begin in the late nineteenth century.

3. **C** Because cities rivaled each other for honors, including athletic honors, it is logical to predict that the people of Kroton resented their hero's defection to another city and destroyed his statues in anger. Nothing in the passage suggests that Astylos considered returning to Kroton (option A), so this is not a predictable outcome. Astylos was already a citizen of Syracuse, so he could not later be denied citizenship (option B). The passage states that the

cities were rivals; it is, therefore, illogical to predict that Kroton and Syracuse merged as an outcome of Astylos's activities (option D).

Lesson 19 Practice (page 53)

1. **B** The tour guide is a big supporter of hydro-dams as an inexpensive and clean form of energy. He would probably like to see more of them around the world. Windmills (option A) are not mentioned in the passage. Hydro-dams use river water, therefore the tour guide wouldn't think it should only be used for drinking (option C). The tour guide talks about the benefits of dams and would therefore not agree with option D.

2. **H** She would probably tell them what she learned as a way of getting them more interested. Trisha probably wouldn't talk about her career plans until she could explain why she thought hydro-dams were important (option F). Trisha was impressed, so she probably wouldn't ignore them (option G). By the end of the story, Trisha didn't have any complaints (option J).

3. **A** The tour guide has a lot of information and knowledge about how hydro-dams convert water to energy. Other types of power plants are not mentioned (option B). The tour guide doesn't say how much electricity is enough (option C). The tour guide doesn't express an opinion about what consumers should or shouldn't do (option D).

4. **H** Trisha marveled at the machinery in the dam. Option F is not correct because Trisha said she would like to work on turbines, and turbines are part of dams. Option G is not correct because Trisha realizes the importance of the turbine in creating electricity. Option J is not correct because Trisha thought about her new computer game during the passage.

Lesson 20 Practice (page 55)

1. **C** The passage states that the invention of the steamboat led to new trading posts, which in turn led to more trading with remote villages. This caused isolated tribes to have increased exposure to the infected goods that were being traded for buffalo hides. The steamboat would make travel easier, not more difficult (option A). Option B is not correct because trading does not usually involve money. The steamboat would not be a source of anger or confrontation among traders (option D); it helped their businesses grow.

2. **G** The passage says that smallpox was brought to North America from Europe. Option F is not correct because the passage states that Europeans were often protected from catching the disease because they had been exposed to it. Exposure had helped them develop a resistance to it. The Native American population did not grow and expand, and the culture did not either (option H). Smallpox was brought across the Atlantic Ocean (option J).

3. **A** The best answer is A because all people, including Native Americans, can now be protected against some diseases by getting vaccinations. Blankets aren't the main cause of the spread of diseases today (option B). Face masks might protect people from some diseases (option C), but it is not the best answer because not all diseases are airborne. Because diseases can be brought to America, staying in America (option D) would not prevent someone from coming into contact with a disease.

Lesson 21 Practice (page 57)

1. **B** Based on the detail that the family is absent when Bingo barks and readers' knowledge that dogs are territorial, Bingo's intention is most likely to protect his territory. Since Bingo barks when the family is away and he is alone, the barking cannot be a welcome (option A). Since the letter implies that Bingo is indoors and the people are outside the Fortune home, it is impossible for Bingo to play with approaching people (option C). Option D does not make sense because indoor dogs are not aware of neighbors in nearby homes and would not bark to call to them.

2. **H** The first sentence in the second paragraph of the letter explains that angry, or upset, neighbors is the effect of Bingo's barking. The letter makes no mention of punishing Bingo (option F) or returning him to the shelter (option J). In the letter, Mr. Fortune relates an incident with dinner guests, so the lack of visitors (option G) is incorrect.

3. **D** Mr. Fortune follows up his recounting of Bingo's pawing with the discovery that his boss's pant leg now has a hole in it. Although readers might predict that a boss, angry about his damaged clothing, might terminate Mr. Fortune's employment (option A), nothing in the letter supports this answer. The letter suggests that Bingo paws people, not the table, so broken dinnerware (option B) is not a logical answer. Although *acid indigestion* (option C) is often an effect of emotional upset or turmoil, it is not mentioned in the letter.

4. F Readers who combine the setting of Bingo's behavior (the dinner table) with prior knowledge that dogs often beg for "people food" conclude that Bingo whines and paws people so they will give him food to eat. Option G is not correct because Mr. Fortune's letter includes no details about people playing with Bingo. The idea that dogs purposely try to punish their owners (option H) inaccurately suggests that dogs experience emotions such as vengeance. Mr. Fortune's description of the dinner table scene contains no words that suggest danger (option J).

Lesson 22 Practice (page 59)

1. D The reason that the author wrote the article is to describe some steps that are useful in finding and getting a job. The author is not telling a story about someone (option A). The part about preparing a resume does not say how to write a resume (option B). The article is written for job seekers, not employers (option C).

2. G The author thinks that readers will be happy with a job that pays well and interests them. The author doesn't try to persuade readers to agree with a particular point of view (option F). The article is intended to help people find a paying position, not a volunteer one (option H). The article doesn't explain how to find the classified section (option J).

3. A Option A is the best answer because it succinctly describes the entire article. Options B and D address only details, while option C is not correct because the article is not about benefits.

4. G The introductory paragraph supports the statement in option G. The entire article is about how preparation will bring results. Options F and H are true, but they are small details, not the big picture. Option J is not correct because it is vague.

Lesson 23 Practice (page 61)

1. C The author calls the umbilical cord's blood a "lifeline," or life-saving treatment, for people who have leukemia. The passage does not mention accident victims (option A). The passage doesn't describe how blood is given to hospital patients (option B) or how umbilical cords are removed from newborn babies (option D).

2. F The author of this passage uses personal testimonial by telling of his or her own experience as a leukemia survivor. The passage does not give a testimonial from an expert (option J) and it does not exaggerate any details (option G). Option H is

incorrect because the author does not use any examples.

3. C The last sentence of the passage explains that 10,000 babies are born every day. Each baby is a "possibility of hope." The passage does not support the statements in options A, B, and D.

4. F Umbilical-cord blood can possibly cure many life-threatening diseases, which is a second chance at life. The passage mentions medical treatments, but does not discuss medicine (option G). It does not address harvesting bone marrow (option H) or ways of giving birth (option J).

Lesson 24 Practice (page 63)

1. D The passage is about the basics of soil. This passage is not about how to cook (option A). It is factual, so it can't be science fiction (option B). It does not report on news or a current event (option C).

2. G This information would likely be found in a book or magazine about gardening. This topic would probably not be found in the newspaper (option F). A textbook on insects would be mostly about insects, not growing vegetables (option H). The topic of improving soil is informational or nonfiction. It wouldn't be found in a fictional novel (option J).

3. A The passage offers information about soil. It does not report news (option B), entertain (option C), or tell a story (option D).

4. G The phrase *need* to in option G expresses an opinion. The author thinks people need to look after and care for soil, but not everyone would agree with this. Options F, H, and J are facts.

TABE Review: Evaluate and Extend Meaning (pages 64–65)

1. B This passage could be found in a magazine that includes book reviews. The passage is about a novel; it is not actually one (option A). Option C is incorrect because the passage doesn't explain how to write; it describes the childhood of a particular writer. The passage is not about the Great Depression; it's about a book that was set during that time period (option D). [Genre]

2. F The author of this review recommends a book to readers. The article does not try to motivate readers to write stories (option G). It doesn't tell how readers can overcome obstacles; it tells us that one woman overcame them (option H). Option J is incorrect because the author only tries to interest, not persuade, readers. [Author's Purpose]

3. **C** The author enthusiastically describes Angelou's life story. Option A contradicts the review, which tells how Maya Angelou does overcome hardships. The author doesn't express an opinion about moving around during childhood (option B). Option D contradicts the positive statements in the review. [Apply Passage Elements]

4. **H** Because Mrs. Flowers helped Angelou, Angelou's gratitude for the woman is a predictable outcome. The passage contains no clues that Flowers adopted Angelou (option F) or that she lent the Angelous money (option G). The passage contains no details that describe interaction between Mrs. Flowers and Maya Angelou's son, Guy (option J). [Predict Outcome]

5. **C** The passage says that Maya Angelou was abused by her mother's boyfriend, so she probably wanted to get as far away from him as possible so he couldn't keep hurting her. Option A is incorrect because Maya must have liked her brother; she changed her name to the nickname he gave her. Option B contradicts the passage; Maya's grandmother "taught her to have pride in herself." Option D contradicts the passage; Maya's son "became the new meaning in her life." [Generalizations]

6. **F** The author illustrates the hardships of Maya Angelou's childhood by giving examples of difficult times in her life, such as leaving home and being abused. The author does not exaggerate the hardships, but just honestly describes them (option G). The author was not a part of Maya Angelou's life so he or she couldn't give a personal testimony about it (option H). There are no experts mentioned in the passage (option J). [Style Techniques]

7. **D** The words "artfully depicts" express the opinion that the author thinks the book is well-written. Options A and B are facts; Maya was happy that she had a baby. It is also a fact that Maya learned lessons about life from her grandmother (option C). [Fact and Opinion]

Performance Assessment: Reading (pages 66–85)

A. **A** Staring into the sun can make it hard to see. Looking at color (option B) and shade (option C) do not affect one's vision. Glasses don't *shine* in people's eyes (option D); they are worn on people's eyes.

B. **J** Dave went to see if there was an intruder in the house. Option F is incorrect because most likely the dog was barking because of the noise. Dave took a baseball bat for protection, not with which to play baseball (option G). He did not know for sure if a window was broken (option H).

1. **C** Time lines sequence key information in an easy-to-reference, visual format. Graphics, such as time lines, that accompany articles reinforce or supplement information in an encyclopedia article; they do not contradict the article (option A). The italicized references immediately following the article title, not the time line, cite other sources of information (option B). Option D is incorrect because authors are not credited in encyclopedias (option D). [Reference Sources]

2. **F** The author explained what logrolling is and why it is a good sport to consider trying. The passage did not tell a logging story (option G). It did not go into detail about how logging camps were run (option H). Option J is incorrect because the author was not trying to convince readers to learn more about how the sport developed. [Author's Purpose]

3. **B** Option B is correct because the passage discusses the physical aspects and mental benefits of logrolling. Option A is not correct because the passage says that people of all backgrounds enjoy logrolling. Option C is not correct because people are interested in logrolling. Option D is not correct because the passage says that some people pick up the sport quickly. [Supporting Evidence]

4. **J** By bending their knees and taking quick steps, logrollers can keep their movement going in order to stay on the log. Bending one's knees will not give a logroller more *power* (option F) or *energy* (option G). Option H is incorrect because *stillness* means motionless or the opposite of *motion*. [Same Meaning]

5. **D** The passage says that it is not a good idea to look at your feet while attempting logrolling. Options A, B, and C are all recommended in the passage. [Details]

6. **H** The winner is the last one standing on the log. The loser is the first one who falls off the log and into the water. Options F and J are incorrect because the goal is to stay on a rolling log, not to roll logs into a river or onto the shore. The goal is to stay on the log the longest, not to be the first one to stand up (option G). [Conclusion]

7. **C** To the left of page 30 is the listing for "laying turf grass." Information about trellises (option A) is found on page 320; information on the unicorn plant (option B) is found on page 350; information about controlling erosion (option D) is found on page 304. [Index]

8. F *See Staking* is listed under the *Supports* heading. Options G, H, and J are incorrect because *Troughs, Planting,* and *Tool Sheds* are not listed under *Supports.* [Index]

9. C Under the topic *Tomatoes,* there is a page number (149) for information about pest and disease control. An insect that eats tomatoes is called a pest. Information about trapping small animals is listed on page 91 (option A). Information about feeding tomatoes is listed on page 145 (option B). Information on toads is listed on page 244 (option D). [Index]

10. J A basic list of tools is found on page 211. Information about growing vegetables in troughs is found on page 135 (option F). Information about planting trees is found on page 158 (option G). Information on tool sheds is found on page 210 (option H). [Index]

11. B The topic "Stems" is not listed on this index page because it comes before *sun* in the alphabet. Options A, C, and D are all listed on this index page. [Index]

12. F The author's point of view is that fire ants are a nuisance. Options G and J are incorrect because they promote the spread of more fire ants, something that the author does not favor. The author probably would not support research on the benefits of fire ants (option H) because he or she reports that they "cause serious harm to people, animals, and crops." [Point of View]

13. C The ants are best known for the fire-like burning sensation that the venom in their bite causes. Option A is not the best answer because the passage did not go into detail about the color shade of the ants. Options B and D are not facts, and are not supported by the passage. [Conclusion]

14. G The passage states that the ants originally came from South America. Therefore, they are not native to the United States. Fire ants are probably not much of a threat to large domestic animals because they don't feed on them (option F). Option H is incorrect because the last paragraph states that small areas of fire ants can be controlled and that there is "hope" for future control of large areas. Option J is incorrect because the passage does not mention that the ants can be trained. [Generalizations]

15. D Fire ants eat ticks, so they could be useful in getting rid of a tick population infesting livestock. Fire ants attack birds (option A) and eat crops such as corn

(option B). Option C is incorrect because the sting of the fire ant hurts humans. [Conclusion]

16. G The passage goes into detail about the aggressive behavior of the fire ants and the pain that their sting creates. Options F and J are incorrect because these are reasons for people to like fire ants. Option H is not the best answer because it is not the main reason that fire ants are a nuisance. [Stated Concepts]

17. C The white blisters that the sting creates can become "infected if not kept clean." Washing the affected area would keep it clean. Rubbing the area (option A) and putting sand on it (option D) might cause further irritation or even infection. Putting ice cubes around the area (option B) would not help to keep it clean. [Conclusion]

18. F The fastest way to find out where the Alabama Gulf Coast is would be to look in an atlas for a map of the state of Alabama. Options G and J are incorrect because these sources don't usually have state maps in them. Option H is not correct because a general travel guide probably wouldn't have a state map of Alabama either. [Reference Sources]

19. B A book called *Recipes for Organic Gardening* would probably have a recipe or instructions on how to make a natural or organic pesticide for gardens. Option A is incorrect because it probably has general information about natural areas. Option C is incorrect because fire ants are not a threat to rivers. A book about beneficial insects (option D) would not describe ways to wipe out or destroy pests such as fire ants. [Reference Sources]

20. G Section 5 describes various utility expenses that the landlord may assume. Section 6 (option F) describes monetary deposits that the lessee (Mai) must make. Similarly, Mai's monthly rental fee is outlined in Section 4 (option H). Section 2 (option J) is an incorrect response because it mentions no fees or charges. [Consumer Materials]

21. A The meaning of the word *let* stems from the concept of "to permit or allow." In this case, the word means "to allow or permit use or occupation of by contract agreement" or "to lease or rent." *Let* denotes usage or temporary occupation of, not display of (option B), donation of (option C), or sale of (option D). [Same Meaning]

22. J According to Section 6, *charges for damages … may be deducted* from the security deposit. Section 5 implies that utilities are already in place (option F). The rental agreement does not mention property tax (option G) or renter's insurance (option H).

Property taxes are the responsibility of the property owner and rental insurance would be the responsibility of the lessee. [Consumer Materials]

23. D Point A describes sublease and lease assignment terms, which require the consent of the landlord. Section 3 (option A) outlines the rental period only, while Point E (option B) describes required property conditions at the time of vacancy. Section 4 (option C) is also an incorrect response, as it describes the monthly rent, not the terms of vacating the property prior to the expiration of the lease. [Consumer Materials]

24. G *Reasonable notice* prevents surprise inspections by requiring the landlord to contact the lessee before entering the apartment. The words *premises* (option F) and *abandonment* (option J) are incorrect because the first refers to the rental property and the second describes the act of leaving without the intention of returning. Option H is also incorrect because prospective, or possible, tenants are not subject to surprise inspections. [Appropriate Word]

25. A Point D states that Mai agrees that she will not *disturb the peace and quiet, maintain a public nuisance,* and *conduct business activities* in or near her apartment. Section 1 (option B) merely specifies the names of the landlord and lessee. Point F (option C) discusses the financial responsibility for court costs if there is a dispute between the landlord and lessee. It does not specify which lessee behaviors are unacceptable. Section 2 (option D) describes the address and furnishings of the rental unit. [Consumer Materials]

26. J The passage is mostly about a girl who spent the night walking around Shanghai and taking in its culture and sights with her uncle John. Option F is incorrect because it has no direct ties to the passage. Option G is incorrect because while the author did walk with her uncle, the passage was focused on Shanghai, not John. Option H is not correct because the story is not about the author's childhood; it is about her present life. Most likely her uncle would not take a child to walk around a city until 2:00 in the morning.

27. A Option A is correct because the first sentence states that she had just walked out of the airport. At the end of the first paragraph, the author calls China a strange land, which indicates she was not familiar with it and had just arrived there. Options B, C, and D are incorrect because they are not supported by the passage.

28. G The author talks about being reverent while at a temple even though she was unfamiliar with the

practices, and although it did not look appetizing, she was willing to try the local food. By the end of the passage, she says she fell in love with China, which indicates a feeling of respect. Option F is not correct because the author only says the salesman she encountered in Shanghai were aggressive; she did not say all salesmen were aggressive. Options H and J are incorrect because they contradict information in the passage.

29. B The author was uncomfortable with strangers being so close to her, and she was uncomfortable with them touching her. Options A and D contradict the passage; the author and John were touched by strangers at least twice, once by a man trying to grab John's wallet and once when a woman touched the author's eyelashes. Option C contradicts the information in the passage.

30. G The author was willing to try to food she saw being cooked on bikes, but she described it as disgusting, dirty, and sour, and she says that it later made her sick. There is no information to support option F. Option H contradicts the information in the passage; the author did try the local food. Option J is not correct because the author did not enjoy the local food and would most likely not want to recreate it.

31. D The author expresses her own personal opinion when she said the kabob tasted dirty and sour. Some people may disagree with her judgment. Options A, B, and C are all facts and based in evidence that can be proven.

32. J The author begins by saying that she hates Shanghai and feels alone, overwhelmed, and lost. By the end of the passage, the author says she fell in the love with the city. Options F, G, and H are incorrect because they do not accurately describe her feelings.

33. A The very first thing that Grandpa Tony did when he got off the boat was enter the building. He didn't mention taking off his coat (option B) and he didn't mention going to a new school (option C). Option D is incorrect because he climbed the steps after entering the building. [Details]

34. H Sophia learned some family history from her mom. Her grandfather's memories are part of the family history. Options F and J are incorrect because Sophia and her grandfather don't mention their travel preferences. Grandpa Tony helps Sophia with her project, but the letters don't mention that Sophia helps others (option G). [Character Aspects]

35. B Grandpa Tony offered to go to Sophia's school to talk with her class. Options A, C, and D are incorrect because Grandpa Tony doesn't give these as reasons to visit Sophia's school. [Stated Concepts]

36. **G** The "golden door" that Grandpa Tony referred to is the Statue of Liberty. Options F and H are incorrect because the "golden door" is not a real door. Option J is not correct because the statue itself symbolizes the opportunity for a better life. [Style Techniques]

37. **D** Sophia wants to *interview* her grandfather or "ask questions" about his experience immigrating to the United States. She doesn't have to meet him to interview him (option A). An interview can be part of a news article, but a *news article* is a noun (option B); the word is used as a verb. Option C is not a correct definition of the word *interview*; *to congratulate* means to "express pleasure at another's good fortune." [Same Meaning]

38. **H** The passage indicates that a crash diet does result in rapid weight loss (though not long-term weight loss). Option F is not correct because it contradicts information in the passage. Option G is not correct because it is a result of a crash diet, but is not the *intention* of a crash diet. Option J is not correct because it is an "ingredient" of a crash diet, but is not the *intention* of a crash diet. [Cause and Effect]

39. **C** The author states that lean muscle burns the most calories. By maintaining a muscle-building program, the body holds on to its lean muscle mass. Option A is incorrect because it contradicts information in the passage. Options B and D are incorrect because the author does not link strength training to the body's water supply. [Stated Concepts]

40. **F** According to the passage, a crash diet results in losing only water weight. Therefore, as soon as the person resumes normal eating habits, the water weight returns. Options G, H, and J are incorrect because they contradict information in the passage. [Cause and Effect]

41. **A** The word *restricting* in this passage means "limiting." It is used to describe diets that limit the number of calories consumed. *Increase* means to make greater, so it means the opposite of *restricting*. Option B is incorrect because *consume* means to eat or use up. Option C is incorrect because *acquire* means to get or take on. Option D is incorrect because *limit* means almost the same thing as *restrict*. [Opposite Meaning]

42. **G** The last paragraph states that you can only be sure that your weight loss is body fat through strength and resistance training and by staying well hydrated. Options F, H, and J are incorrect because they contradict the advice that the author gives on how to lose body fat. [Apply Passage Elements]

43. **D** The author advises readers to lose fat and states that staying hydrated and increasing one's lean muscle through strength training helps to achieve this. Option A contradicts the passage. Options B and C are incorrect because they are single statements from the passage; they are not a complete summary. [Summary]

44. **F** The blues is one style of music for which Ray Charles is famous. The article could be found in a magazine of that genre. An introductory book on classical music (option G) would not have a biography of Ray Charles's life because he does not play that style of music. Option H is incorrect because the main theme of the passage is not political. Option J is incorrect because it is more of a biography about a particular person than a paper about general racial injustice. [Genre]

45. **D** Ray Charles refused to do a segregated show because he was opposed to the racial injustice he experienced while on tour. Ray Charles is best known for recording many styles of music, not just country and western music (option A). Options B and C are incorrect because they contradict information in the passage. [Character Aspects]

46. **F** The fourth paragraph explains that studying classical music gave Ray Charles the opportunity to learn how to write and arrange music. Option G is not correct because he wasn't particularly interested in becoming a classical musician. Option H is not correct because he did not want it to end. He wanted to take the opportunity to learn so that he could move on to writing and arranging blues and jazz. Option J is not correct because he got something out of studying classical music that he could apply to the music in which he was more interested. [Conclusion]

47. **A** Ray acted on a *pledge* or a promise to King's cause. Options B and D are incorrect because they do not mean the same as *commitment*. *Calling* and *yearning* are feelings of longing to do something. Option C is incorrect because *witness* means to "observe or testify." [Same Meaning]

48. **J** The passage described the racial inequality and segregation that Ray experienced at restaurants and gas stations. Ray was not amused or overjoyed by the treatment (options F and H). Ray was angry,

but not because of the food (option G). [Stated Concepts]

49. D The passage did not state that Ray ever went to jail. It stated that he raised money for people who went to jail because of unfair laws. Options A, B, and C are incorrect because each of these family members died during Ray's life. [Details]

50. H The passage is about Ray's personal struggles and his triumph through music. The other options are incorrect because they are not true. Ray did not record classical music (option F). The passage did not mention that he joined protest rallies (option G). Ray Charles did not write books about his family (option J). [Summary]

51. C The details of the last paragraph suggest that sleep disorders are serious medical conditions; consulting a doctor is a predictable outcome for concerned readers. While people with sleep disorders may eventually change jobs (option A) to remove the cause of their sleep problems, the passage mentions nothing about job changes. Simply reading a passage about sleep disorders would not help someone with a sleep disorder to sleep more (option B). Option D is not supported by the passage; no mention is made of beds as contributing factors in sleep disorders. [Predict Outcome]

52. F The word *promising* connotes a pledge or hope for the future. *Depressing* (option G) is the opposite of a word that gives people hope; rather, it implies a hopeless or despairing state. *Cunning* (option H) means "sly or wily," and *taxing* means "causing

physical exertion"; neither word completes the idea of hope. [Appropriate Word]

53. C Paragraph 3 of the article describes sleep interruptions caused by periods of breathing stoppage. Options A and B refer to other sleep disorders. Daylight interrupts the sleep of night-time workers, while leg discomfort disturbs people with restless legs syndrome. Although the article asserts that emotional problems are one cause of sleep disorders (option D), no specific mention is made of sleep interruptions caused by these problems.

54. F Paragraph 1 reveals that sleep disorders result from *physical or emotional illness or disease* and certain situations. Option G is incorrect; according to paragraph 1, nearly one in every four Americans has sleep difficulties. The response that doctors are unconcerned (option H) is also inaccurate; the last line of the article reveals that the medical community is conducting ongoing research to discover new treatments and cures for sleep disorders. Nothing in the article suggests that people can treat their own sleep disorders, so option J is incorrect. [Cause and Effect]

55. D The word *ongoing* means "continuing or chronic," so this is the opposite of the word *occasional,* which implies a temporary status. The word *continuing* (option A) means the same as *ongoing,* not the opposite. *Delightful* (option B) means pleasurable; it does not address the length of an experience. The word *trivial* (option C) means unimportant; it is not a measure of time or